SET FORTH YOUR CASE

SET FORTH YOUR CASE

Studies in Christian Apologetics

CLARK H. PINNOCK

MOODY PRESS • CHICAGO

For the tough-minded,
who also love the truth

Copyright 1967 by Craig Press
Moody Press Edition 1971

Library of Congress Catalog Number 67-29598

ISBN: 0-8024-7850-6

Third Printing, 1972
Fourth Printing, 1972
Fifth Printing, 1973
Sixth Printing, 1974
Seventh Printing, 1975
Eighth Printing, 1976

Printed in the United States of America

CONTENTS

INTRODUCTION

IT IS ONE MARK OF THE TRUTH of our holy religion that it courts enquiry. Christianity lays open its claim to every one that asks a reason of the hope which it inspires, and declines no species of a fair investigation."[1] Thus wrote Daniel Wilson in 1829 before an antirational temper became dominant in our culture. The defense of the faith belongs to the preaching of the gospel. Preaching without apologetics is scarcely preaching at all. It encourages naked credulity and shallow conviction. Christian and non-Christian alike demand to know, and have a *right* to know, that the historical and intellectual foundations beneath the gospel are sound. In Isaiah 41:21, the Lord issues a ringing challenge to the false gods: "SET FORTH YOUR CASE, says the LORD; bring your proofs, says the King of Jacob" (RSV). Certainly the Lord Himself does not shrink from the demand for authenticating credentials on the part of the gospel. Our good news is an accredited claim and bona fide offer. Our confidence in its objective truth is reflected in our zeal for its defense and proclamation.

"Be ready always to give an answer to every man that asketh you a reason of the hope that is in you, with meekness and fear" (1 Pe 3:15). All Christians

7

stand beneath this command, but many are disobedient
to it. The earliest believers called men to an intelligent faith. They pressed boldly the claims of Jesus
Christ as they had been dramatically verified in history
by the fact of the resurrection. Upon the validity of
this historical datum rested and continues to rest the
truth of the Christian message. In describing his witness, the apostle Paul wrote of its two faces: "For we
are unto God a sweet savour of Christ, in them that
are saved, and in them that perish: to the one we are
the savour of death unto death; and to the other the
savour of life unto life" (2 Co 2:15-16). Our task
includes law and gospel, a warning and an invitation,
good news and bad, despair and hope. The negative
side of the coin consists in a radical unmasking of the
natural man who is trapped in the prison of an impersonal universe, playing a role in a drama without
a plot. The positive side involves a display of the total
evidence which verifies and validates the Christian
truth claim, together with a rebuttal of criticisms directed against it.

The shape of our defense is to some extent molded
by the intellectual climate of our times. The apologist
needs to be wise in his generation, and play the matter
by ear. For there is no normative approach to Christian apologetics. Our aim requires a continual refocus-
ing simply because our target moves ceaselessly. We
have a responsibility to reach our generation. Although
we may learn much from the wisdom of the ages, the
moment fresh thought begins to wane, our witness
becomes stale and irrelevant. This book has been written for believers in Christ who desire to witness intelligently and effectively for Him, and who feel the
heavy pressure from the current nonchristian consensus
with its relativism and loss of absolutes and, ironically,

simultaneously from the existentialist theology with its fatal emphasis on subjective irrationalism.

The Christian gospel pleases both heart and head. It is a rational and intelligent faith. Therefore, it cannot be presented on the spur of the moment without much reflective thought, in the spouting of proof texts and an appeal to religious excitement in the soul. There is a need for more serious regard for the philosophical and factual structure of the gospel so that a bolder and more imaginative witness can be undertaken in this critical hour. May God grant a new reformation in truth for the church, and use this document to produce a substantial deepening in our understanding of the Christian faith.

It is an old saying that to steal from one writer is plagiarism, to steal from many is research, and to be inspired by any and all writers is creativity! Indebtedness could be acknowledged to many for the thoughts in this book, but must be directed to one, Dr. Francis A. Schaeffer, L'Abri Fellowship, Huémoz, Switzerland, a man valiant for truth. A mighty book requires a mighty theme. The grandeur of our theme is beyond dispute. Our prayer is that the book itself might lend glory to the Lord, and encourage the people of God to undertake a bold witness for Him which will shake the foundations of our tottering, secular culture. May the Holy Spirit use the book to that end.

1

THE LEGITIMACY OF
CHRISTIAN APOLOGETICS

CHRISTIAN APOLOGETICS is concerned with a defense of the truthfulness of the Christian religion. The task of theology is to define the content of revealed truth, while the task of apologetics is to defend its validity. Theology and apologetics are twin members of a common family. In our spiritual warfare, the one is defensive, the other offensive. The aim of apologetics is not to trick a person into becoming a Christian against his will. It strives rather at laying the evidence for the Christian gospel before men in an intelligent fashion so that they can make a meaningful commitment under the convicting power of the Holy Spirit. The heart cannot delight in what the mind rejects as false. Apologetics presents compelling reasons to the mind for receiving Christ as Saviour into the total man. Faith is based upon credible evidence which people can recognize as trustworthy in accord with proper criteria for truth.

The Greek word *apologia* from which we derive *apologetics* occurs some eight times in the New Testament. It signifies a defense of conduct and procedure. Several times the apostle Paul was called upon in a court of law to defend his right to preach the gospel in public (Ac 22:1; 2 Ti 4:16). Festus made the sense

clear when he told King Agrippa of his conviction that
an accused prisoner deserves the right to make his
defense in the presence of his accusers and in a court
of law (Ac 25:16). The *apologia* Peter commands us
to render (1 Pe 3:15) is not primarily in the face of
police inquiry; the verb "ask" rather suggests an in-
formal question such as "Why are you a Christian?"
To such a query every believer is obliged to be ready
with a sensible answer. To assist in framing a convincing answer is the purpose of this book. Modern man
is confronted by a bewildering array of clues to the
meaning of the universe. Choosing Christ to be his
ultimate clue is not an arbitrary act of desperation,
but an intelligent step of faith based on good and
sufficient evidences. The aim of apologetics is to
demonstrate the validity of the Christian system and
defend it against attack.

However, the noble discipline of apologetics has
fallen upon hard times recently. For its two implacable
foes have reared their heads. On the one hand, rationalism has never left much room for supernatural
revelation and miraculous incarnation, and finds
apologetics beneath its dignity. If the Christian faith
consists merely of intuitive truths and ethical codes,
to defend the case for supernatural Christianity is
rather beside the point. On the other hand, mysticism
with its delight in the empty irrationalism of the heart
disdains apologetics as impertinent and unnecessary.
Certainly the neoorthodox theology would disown the
term *mystical* to describe itself, but it is appropriate
nonetheless for designating this facet of its thought.
For the basic thesis of the dialectical theology is that
the acts of God in history cannot be detected apart
from a leap of faith, and the revealed words of God
cannot ever be identified with any words. Divine acts

are beyond history and divine words beyond language. Faith in Christ becomes an arbitrary act grounded in nothing. The gospel itself may be devoid of historical fact and objective truth, but this is no concern to "faith," according to the new theology. God might even be dead as some have alleged, and one could never be sure in the absence of any decisive proofs for His existence. Indeed, the radical forms of the neo-orthodox theology are admirably suited to survive the death of God, because this word *god* describes only an existential relationship, and not the self-contained triune God of Scripture. A casual reading of the New Testament is enough to show how foreign to the gospel are these religious constructions. The very essence of the good news is the claim that in Christ Jesus God openly showed Himself in the empirical realm of history, and on that basis He commands all men everywhere to repent (Jn 1:14; 1 Jn 1:1-3; Ac 17:31). The incarnation had a soteriological purpose—the name of Jesus, not the intuitive truths of reason, saves —and it had an epistemological purpose—the "unknown God" is no longer unknown. There are checking procedures for testing the Christian clue, and it is the task of apologetics to present the fruits of them cogently.

Christian commitment does not take place in a vacuum. What modern unbelief needs is not less apologetics but more. Faith is *not* the opposite of knowledge. The scandal of the gospel is *not* its alleged immunity from proof. The gospel makes sense, not non-sense. Its offense lies in its moral unmasking of the sinner, not in its supposed uncertain truthfulness. The mind is not to be left at the threshold in Christianity. Such deliberate irrationalism is positively anti-Christian and plays directly into the hands of un-

believers who cherish the illusion that the gospel is a
foolish leap of faith. "The greater the risk, the greater
the faith" is one of the most damaging fallacies ever
to afflict the mind of Christian people. It leaves men
secure in their false world views, and denies them
access to the public evidences which make the gospel
unique. Modern theology has rejected "magic" for
"myth" and modern man will believe neither. The hour
has struck for a virile apologetic which will challenge
the naive confidence of humanism and display the
beauty of the Christian system. We will never win a
victory if we decline to enter the conflict. The current
apologetic strategy of retreating from all positions
under attack may avoid bloodshed, but can result
only in abject surrender and total defeat.

Ironically enough, a definite species of irrationalism
also appears in branches of Protestant orthodoxy. Because of an unbiblical appeal to the testimony of the
Holy Spirit in the heart, an unholy alliance of skeptics
and Christians together disparages the solid defenses
of the gospel. As if the faith which the Spirit com-
mends to the heart must be an irrational faith! Is it
not almost blasphemous, these Christians ask, to seek
to make the gospel acceptable to the natural man?
Can debate and argument ever really convert anyone?
Do they not lead to endless wrangling and heresy?

This confusion arises through a failure to distinguish
the inner from the outer testimony in the gospel. A
Christian preacher or witness brings the data of Christ
and His work to a person. Theology and apologetics
join hands in performing this essential role in evangelism. However, apart from the work of the Spirit,
the gospel will fall upon deaf ears. The problem lies
in the inability of the natural man (1 Co 2:14), not
in the veracity of the gospel (2 Co 4:3-4). Conver-

sion takes place when our witness to the truth, and the Spirit's creative work in the heart coincide (Ac 16:14). The inner and the outer witness are essential for nailing down certitude. The spirit employs our witness as a *tool* in regenerating the heart (1 Pe 1:23). The "foolishness" of the gospel (1 Co 1:21) is not the offense it renders to the *ratio* (reason) of man, but to his *hubris* (presumptuous pride). The gospel dissolves all his sand castles, and bursts all his balloons. But *in itself* the gospel is perfectly intelligible, consistent and satisfying.

It is surely a delight as a Christian to reflect upon and appropriate the rich verities of Christian revelation. But at a certain point it is imperative to ask whether the grand assumption, Jesus Christ is Lord, is true or false, legitimate or fanciful. Theology-in-a-circle is an interesting intellectual pursuit no doubt, but it has no compelling relevance to the world unless its subject matter is reliable. Obviously, Paul plants, Apollos waters, and God gives the increase (1 Co 3:6). But it does not follow that the seed is not fertile and the water nonirrigating in its effects. In salvation the Spirit creates the *capacity* for receiving God's truth, but *truth* it is. In producing a photograph, light must fall upon the film, and the film must be processed to yield an impression. Both light and development are essential to a photograph. In precisely the same way the Spirit and evidences are essential to saving faith. To cite a telling phrase of B. B. Warfield,

> One might as well say that photography is independent of light, because no light can make an impression unless the plate is prepared to receive it. The Holy Spirit does not work a blind, an ungrounded faith in the heart. What is supplied by his creative energy in working faith is not a ready-made

faith, rooted in nothing, and clinging without reason to its object; nor yet new grounds of belief in the object present; but just a new ability of the heart to respond to the grounds of faith, sufficient in themselves, already present to the understanding. We believe in Christ because it is rational to believe in him, not though it be irrational. For the birth of faith in the soul, it is *just as essential* [italics added] that grounds of faith should be present to the mind as that the Giver of faith should act creatively upon the heart.[1]

Certainly the Bible teaches that the sinner is deaf, blind and dead to the claims of the gospel. But this does not absolve us of the responsibility to present truth which can save under the power of the Holy Spirit (cf. Eze 37:1-14). What saves is the Spirit acting upon the data to bring about saving faith.

Psychologically there is no common ground between Christian and non-Christian, in that the latter will not yield to the force of the evidence for the gospel, but will seek to equivocate its thrust. This fact does not relieve us of the duty of presenting it to him prayerfully. The incarnation means that God has supplied data for His existence and character on which an intelligent faith commitment can be made. "The same works that I do bear witness of me, that the Father hath sent me," said Jesus (Jn 5:36). The facts backing the Christian claim are not a special kind of religious fact. They are the cognitive, informational facts upon which all historical, legal and ordinary decisions are based. Confidence in the factual truth of the gospel is simply logical incarnationalism. The fact of Christ can be shared with men without apology.

At the same time there is no place for arrogance and pride. Even the soundest apologetic has no power to make a man a Christian, or coerce a sinner to repent. The Spirit alone has the task of conviction to perform (Jn 16:8-9). But the conviction the Spirit engenders is itself grounded in evidence. The faith by which we shall overcome the world is anchored and rooted in the objective validity of God's acts and words. There is, however, no room for confidence in the flesh. The natural man has a deep-set bias against the gospel (Ro 8:8). All our pleading and argument will do nothing to budge him from his usurped throne of self-worship. The gospel must be "caught" as well as "taught." Even where the soundest evidence conceivable is present to the mind, and faith follows (as with Peter in Mt 16:16), it is no credit to human intelligence. "For flesh and blood hath not revealed it unto thee, but my Father" (v 17). We are instruments in the Spirit's grasp. Without His skill no lasting results ensue. Yet, paradoxically, without the preacher and apologist the Spirit is silent (Ro 10:14-17). The inner event originates with the Spirit, and the outer event originates with us. We are commanded to perform *our* task, not His, and this task includes Christian apologetics.

A sound grasp of Christian apologetics is an indispensable tool for evangelism. From philosopher to peasant the same questions are asked which differ only in the degree of sophistication. An intelligent Christian ought to be able to point up the flaws in a nonchristian position and to present facts and arguments which tell in favor of the gospel. The artist and the farmer have great need of Christ. If our apologetic prevents us from explaining the gospel to any person, it is an inadequate apologetic.

The need for apologetics has become more urgent with the rise of a monolithic secularism. It is a vanish-

ing sector of people who can still be approached with
proof texts and historic Christian terminology. As the
gap between the gospel and our culture widens, the
bridges have to be longer and stronger. Apologetics
deals in the area of *pre*-evangelism. A twenty-minute
sermon with three illustrations and a tearful invitation
is simply insufficient grounds for requesting an intelligent decision for Christ. The total Christian understanding of the world plus the evidences on which
that understanding rests form a necessary deposit of
knowledge which the Christian needs to master. Our
problem does not stem from the insufficiency of gospel
truth but from the increasing distance of unbelievers
from it. Our situation calls for rugged conviction and
boldness. Recent failure to bridge the gap between
orthodoxy and modern agnosticism has been due to
the sheer laziness of Evangelicals to relate their treasure with intellectual courage to the questions being
asked. Biblical truths are weapons in a spiritual warfare, and are capable of being wielded with great effect
by a man of God. But they have grown rusty and dull
for want of use.

Apologetics is related to worship too. It is always
a joyous discovery to see afresh the adequacy and
firmness of God's truth. Christian worship is far removed from the dark cathedrals, flickering candles,
and mystical experiences. It arises in the soul fixed
in adoration and contemplation of God's truth. In-
telligibility is of the essence. The feeling that results
from a tiring spiritual conflict in witness for Christ is
not exultation in the flesh, but renewed amazement
at the beauty of the good news!

Man has always been confronted by a cafeteria of
clues to the meaning of the universe. His choice of the
absolute ground of meaning, by which he orders the

vast diversity of reality encountered, is a religious commitment. His problem is how to choose between the tempting alternatives. The discipline of Christian apologetics exists to assist him to see that the gospel of Jesus Christ is a live option; even more, that it alone can verify its claims, deliver him from despair, and provide solid ground beneath his feet.

2

THE BIG SELLOUT

THERE IS A KEY that unlocks the door to an understanding of modern theology and explains current hostility to Christian apologetics. Once this structural principle is grasped, enormous light is shed on previously inscrutable problems of interpretation. Pitfalls and booby traps can be avoided with ease. The key is the "upper story" pattern in contemporary theology. By this device theology is calculated to survive even the "death of God" itself. But in actuality the price of this sellout is the complete demise of Christian apologetics.

In order to comprehend how theology moved into this position, two cultural facts must be carefully noted.

The Death of Hope and Romanticism

Basic to the humanistic mentality of Western man since the Renaissance has been the belief in the inherent goodness of man and inevitability of his progress. These grand assumptions have been shattered and widely abandoned because of the shocking revelations of man's inhumanity to man in the twentieth century, and the slow realization of the fundamental hopelessness of a naturalistic philosophy. Romanticism still survives in pockets, of course, but the drift of our culture is in the other direction. This intellectual development of our times has created a crisis of meaning.

The Shift to Mysticism

In order to escape from the unpleasant implications of humanism which tend toward nihilism and despair, there has been a deliberate shift to a nonrational solution to the problem of meaning. The facts of history and the bleak logic of the nonchristian world view were found to strangle man's aspirations. So rather than surrender his *rationalism* (the ultimate autonomy of man's mind), man prefers to give up his *rationality* (his logical approach to things). Whereas his head cannot conceive an optimistic answer to his dilemma, his heart comes across with an intuition that saves the day. He *knows* this accidental collocation of atoms we call a world has no meaning, yet he chooses to *believe* in a meaning he creates for himself. The prominence of the existential mood today is only explicable on the basis that it allows man to have logical absurdity without any stigma.

The greatest single tragedy in modern theology is the failure to challenge this secular shift to irrationalism at its foundations. Instead theology has largely moved in exactly the same direction. It too has accepted the unthinkable, namely, a divided field of knowledge with mystical intuition as the clue to reality.

The "lower story," according to the new theology, is the realm of cause and effect, where man confronts brute facts in their great plurality, and functions logically and rationally. This realm is supposed to yield no meaning, no ultimate clue to things. It is necessary to go upstairs to the "upper story" for meaning. The upper level is the field of intuition, faith and conjecture. It is in no way related to or connected

The Divided Field of Knowledge

UPPER STORY

The nonrational, nonlogical, paradoxical, symbolic, untestable, unverifiable, suprahistorical, imaginative, surreal

Impenetrable Concrete Slab

LOWER STORY

The rational, logical, historical, factual, real, testable, verifiable, empirical, provable, scientific.

with the lower level. It is a state of non-mind, the region of the nonrational mystical experience into which LSD users escape with considerable relief. For it enables people to stamp out reality as it is actually experienced and substitute a cerebral paradise of one's own creation. Instead of challenging our culture with the distinctive feature of the gospel, namely, its objective historical base (Jn 1:14), modern theology has jumped on the bandwagon on its way to a fool's paradise.

Let us pause to consider briefly a few examples of how the upper-story theology works. Basically the subject who has faith becomes all-important, while the object of his faith is rather inconsequential. The person of Jesus, for example, is known as a contemporary symbol, embodying some ideal He is supposed to epitomize, but insofar as He is considered a historical individual, His identity is shrouded in deep darkness. In the lower story, historical criticism is said to yield only a human prophet who preached the end of the world; while by an upper-story leap of faith it is possible to raise him to divine significance. By this device it becomes possible to identify "Christ" with whatever modern ideal we wish. For the Nazi theologians (e.g., Kittel and Hirsch) the Christ was indistinguishable from the force of social change found in national socialism. Because liberal theology gave up the standard of historical revelation it became prey to a satanic Christ. The confession "Jesus Christ is Lord" has come to mean almost nothing in our day because of the upper-story mentality.

The same pattern is easily discernible in the approach to Scripture in the "new theology" (viz., the theology which espouses a divided field of knowledge). The Bible is placed in the lower story—a victim of scientific criticism, and yielding no evidence of its divinity. The "word of God" is put in the upper story —a nonverbal, nonrational, mystical, noncommunicative "revelation." The "encounter with God" takes place, we are told, in the upper story. As a human document, the Bible is fallible and errant; as a medium of "revelation" it is inspired. As much could be said for the Koran, Shakespeare, and *Das Kapital*. No weight is given to the uniquely revelatory character of Scripture in the teachings of Jesus and His apostles. But by this neat device, a person can retain the skepticism of a Strauss in one part of his brain (the lower story), and the faith of a Luther in the other.

And if anyone catches on to what you are doing, the cover-up trick is to turn pious. Simply identify reason with works, and the empty imagination with faith, and your critic will go away! By the death of such noble terms, Satan has won many a battle.

The upper-story device applies to many other areas of Christian doctrine. In the doctrine of creation, the method is to put all the biblical teaching upstairs in the region of "faith." By this means, the theologian can jump on the bandwagon of whatever the current scientific consensus happens to be, and appear terribly enlightened. At the same time, creation comes to mean "this is how *I* see the universe." No heads are bumped, a concordat is worked out with the scientist, and everyone gets prizes! Meanwhile the biblical teaching about the origin of things goes unnoticed and unheeded.

Biblical miracles can be neatly sidestepped by using this device. The miracle occurs in the *seeing* of faith, not in the *fact* of history. A miracle is the interpretation which believing people gave to an event which touched them deeply. Israel made a lucky escape from the delta of Egypt, and cried "Yahweh!" The word for God served to satisfy their desire to express their gratitude. But nothing happened that would shock the naturalist. The water from the rock, the quails, the manna, crossing the sea of reeds—all these are put down to "faith." The miracles of the Bible do not prove God exists as they claim to, but merely that people *believed* He did. Again the upper-story device protects the new theologian from all criticism from the side of historical and scientific fact. If the modern secular universities ever decide to eliminate their departments of religion, it will not be because they believe in the supernatural, but because their whole

stance is irrationalistic and offensive of the demands
of an empirical age.

A theologian who is quick on his feet can manage
to dodge almost every objection that has ever been
hurled against the Christian faith by taking refuge in
the upper story. Take the resurrection of Christ, for
example. By faith we confess that God raised Jesus
from the dead. This faith is taken to be an upper-story
commitment, barring any possible testing procedures.
This means, in effect, that the event was not "public,"
and that, if a reporter from the *Jerusalem Post* had
been covering the event of the resurrection, he would
have detected no irregularities in the death and burial
of Jesus. Indeed, according to the new theology, belief
in the resurrection is the province of the psychiatrist
(why did the disciples believe it?) rather than the
historian (what really happened?). Resurrection is an
upper-story belief. There is no way to know whether
it happened or not, except by believing it did.

The upper-story enables a theologian to talk about
the fallenness of man without believing in a literal
Adam. The "fall" is put up-stairs in the area of
"meaning," and Adam is left downstairs in the
shrouded world of fact and truth. Again a Christian
doctrine is detached from the world of factuality and
rationality, and isolated in the sealed capsule of
arbitrary faith. The upper-story symbols are in no way
subject to verification or falsification, and their content is not fixed. The subject who has faith simply
loads these symbols with the meaning he chooses in
accord with the secular mood of his day. The cross is
an example of a contentless symbol in the new
theology. The cross is a constant theme, but the blood
is never mentioned except in scorn. All the "theories"
of atonement are put downstairs. What precisely Jesus

did for us is not explained. The cross means whatever
the interpreter wants it to mean. If he can extract its
meaning from the Bible in some way, so much the
better; but, if he cannot, nothing is lost. For it is the
contemporary Christ who saves, they say. The cross
can mean anything from love to hate, from humility to
a toasted cheese sandwich. The same goes for the
deity of Christ. His divine names, Lord, Son of God,
Son of Man, are given emotional value, without
metaphysical significance. These are taken to be
upper-story designations, terms which express someone's ultimate reference point, or the things of highest
value to him. The doctrine of the Trinity in the upper-
story theology becomes purely a metaphorical description of God produced by men who saw redemptive
history that way. If we attempt to take it as literally
true, it becomes a mathematical absurdity due to the
failure to interpret the Bible existentially. The Bible-
believing Christian has never been confronted by so
clever a device before. But, if he will take the time
to master this divided field of knowledge trick, he will
find himself in a good position to counter it.

The upper-story pattern in theology has only recently come to prominence, but it is by no means new.
It has deep roots in European theology since the
Renaissance. Lessing preferred inner certainty over
the relative uncertainty of historical events. Theologians have been trying to jump over Lessing's "ugly
ditch" ever since. Kant made the dichotomy between
faith and reason, between the noumenal and the
phenomenal worlds, and thrust a thick wedge between
religion and reality. Kierkegaard made the antithesis
very explicit by sharply opposing faith and reason. He
is most directly responsible for the new theology, but
is not its only architect. Oddly enough the new

theology with its upper story is a child of *both* rationalism and existentialism insofar as both movements dislike history. They dislike it also for much the same
reason; namely, because historical fact is not sufficiently certain enough to support faith. From that
point the two movements separate, rationalism moving into scientific humanism, and existentialism moving into the upper-story pattern. But both reject the
biblical claim that what God did in history *is* a sufficient ground for decision and faith. It is antibiblical
to insulate the gospel from the acid baths of historical
criticism. It can stand the investigation, providing the
prejudices are left at home. This dichotomy between
faith and fact is fatal to Christianity and opposed to
the entire biblical witness. It is time it was exposed
once and for all as a cul-de-sac.

The upper story in modern theology is diabolically
clever. The layman should not be surprised if theology
often seems to him ambiguous and ambivalent. For
the first time in history, theology has taken ambiguity
into the heart of its system. The upper-story is a
sophisticated way of retaining the Christian symbols,
while at the same time denying them content and
verifiability. The secular humanist can find refuge in
this pseudo gospel without ever relinquishing his hold
on his naturalism. The new theology is effective in
the churches because it cynically manipulates the
Christian symbols which are deeply rooted in the
memory of the people, and subtly empties them of
all definable content. The congregation has already
lost its power before it comes to realize, if it ever
does, just what has happened, for when X is a symbol
for Y, and Y a symbol for Z, and Z a symbol for X
—things do become rather hard to follow! The big
sellout in modern theology comes at the point of the

complete elimination of the sovereignty of God. His existence is hidden and shadowy; His saving acts are concealed and equivocal; His revelation is subjective and ambiguous; His Christ is an elusive phantom; His laws are open to amendment; His Word is subject to error. God is made to be impotent, unable to command men to repent on the basis of powerful arguments (Ac 17:31), capable only of peeking out from the curtains offstage, hoping some will respond. When this line of thought is taken to its logical conclusions, it seems apparent that the word *God* is only a word. It stands for a certain subjective state in man. God is a relationship, nothing more. Man feels the need for meaning, and cries "God," but he never can know until the end of his days whether this "God" is really there. It is equally possible that no god is there. The upper-story route in contemporary theology is a dead-end street. It leads as surely to despair as naturalism does. Only the road is longer getting there. Classical liberalism was a dangerous but easily detectible foe of historic Christianity. But the new theology is a slippery customer and has managed to come up with a closer counterfeit of the gospel. On that account it is more dangerous.

The effect of the upper story in theology is the complete destruction of apologetics and evidences. There is left absolutely no way to challenge the non-Christian to receive Jesus Christ. Theology has been converted to *solipsism,* the view that reality is whatever the individual makes it. The three descending steps to the abyss are clear: first, subjectivism (religion is all the way you see it), second, relativism (it doesn't matter how you see it), and third, agnosticism (no one has the answer). Solipsism is a nice way to describe modern theology. Insanity is appropriate but less kind. Whatever we call it, the new theology can lead us nowhere, and we had better find a different route.

3

THE RADICAL UNMASKING

ONE OF THE BEST-KEPT SECRETS from the public at large in the twentieth century has been the death of hope and the loss of the human. From every direction —from painting, music, literature, theater, films—an avalanche of testimony has been building up, grimly announcing man's agonizing dilemma in this post-Nietzschean epoch of the decomposition of his gods. In Christian apologetics, as in theology, the law is preached before the gospel in order that the unregenerate man will be exposed and unmasked before the demands of a holy God, and directed to the road of grace. The wicked are like chaff (Ps 1:4-6), they have no valid starting point for their thinking (Pr 1:7), and the foundation of their habitation is sand (Mt 7:26). No flesh can boast in the presence of God (1 Co 1:29; Ro 3:19-20). Indeed, the emperor in the ancient legend, despite all of his pomposity and pride, had no clothes. So it is with modern man if he continues to bypass the redemption which is in Christ Jesus.

In this latter third of the twentieth century, it is apparent that the once-proud dogmas of optimistic humanism are dead and buried. Belief in the inevitability of progress and the innate goodness of man has been replaced by a mood of cynicism and despair.

Oswald Spengler wrote: "Mankind has no aim, no idea, no plan, any more than a family of butterflies or orchids." History is endlessly repetitious, having neither progress nor ultimate goal. Spengler's melancholy was shared by two fellow historians, H. G. Wells and Edward Gibbon. In 1939, near the close of his life, a disillusioned Wells wrote:

> There is no creed, no way of life left in the world at all, that really meets the need of the time . . . there is no reason whatever to believe that the order of nature has any greater bias in favour of man than it had in favour of the ichthyosaur or the pterodactyl. In spite of all my desperation to a brave looking optimism, I perceive that now the universe is bored with him, is turning a hard face to him, and I see him being carried less and less intelligently and more and more rapidly, suffering as every ill-adapted creature must suffer in gross and detail, along the stream of fate, to degradation, suffering and death.

Gibbon came to much the same conclusion when he admitted that history is "little more than the register of the crimes, follies and misfortunes of mankind."

The root problem of the nonchristian humanist is the sheer pointlessness of existing in a godless world. The director of the British Humanist Association, H. J. Blackham, admitted that "the most drastic objection to humanism is that it is too bad to be true." Bertrand Russell summed it up with characteristic eloquence:

> That man is the product of causes which had no prevision of the end they were achieving; that his origin, his growth, his hopes and fears, his loves and his beliefs, are but the outcome of accidental collocations of atoms; that no fire, no heroism, no intensity of thought and feeling, can preserve an individual

life beyond the grave; that all the labour of the ages,
all the devotion, all the inspiration, all the noonday
brightness of human genius, are destined to extinction
in the vast death of the solar system, and that the
whole temple of Man's achievement must inevitably
be buried beneath the debris of a universe in ruins—
all these things, if not quite beyond dispute, are yet so
nearly certain, that no philosophy which rejects them
can hope to stand. Only within the scaffolding of
these truths, only on the firm foundation of unyield-
ing despair, can the soul's habitation henceforth be
safely built.[1]

Testimonies of this kind from non-Christians awakening
to the logic of their own position could be added from
an unnumbered host—from Sartre, Camus, Heidegger,
Durant, Voltaire, Strauss and many more. The un-
bounded optimism of Western man has reached exhaustion, and he faces his own extinction in his own
manufactured hell.

This despair is vividly portrayed in the writings of
Franz Kafka. In his novels and short stories Kafka
gives literary expression to the philosophy of Friedrich
Nietzsche. Kafka is a modern man. His gods have
disappeared and his men are dying. His foothold in
reality is based upon the conviction that there is no
foothold possible. In all his work, *The Castle, The
Trial, America,* anguish and ambiguity are at the
heart of things. The future is always bleak, impenetrable and menacing. A heavy pall of sadness
hangs over everything. He leaves his reader alone in
the cold, black, wintry night. The senseless fatality
of his characters is rooted in the empty futility which
life in a godless world must inherit. Kafka knows no
dancing at the tomb of God. He turns aside and weeps.

This sense of metaphysical despair receives a full
exposition in the "theatre of the absurd" movement.

This group of playwrights, including Samuel Beckett, Eugene Ionesco, Harold Pinter and Jean Genet, has dedicated itself to depicting the absolute emptiness of life. They achieve this aim by employing an effective technique—the use of nonsense language. By dramatically altering the structure of normal language and syntax, these writers create an *experience* of absurdity in the audience. The "absurd" may be defined as the disparity seen between the world as it actually is and the world as it was hoped to be. The clock of hope has run down. Without his metaphysical roots, nonchristian man is effectively lost and drained of the purpose to live. He is an accidental scrap of life surrounded by death. Instead of arguing for the meaninglessness of man's existence, these writers simply *present* it. The breakdown of language in *Waiting for Godot* or *The Bald Soprano,* for example, is intended to indicate the breakdown in all significant existence and communication. At the root of man's existence is nothingness. Man's dreams are in wreckage and ruin. There are no exits from the nonchristian world. Life is a dead-end street. The theater has become an eloquent vehicle for presenting today's dilemma. Beckett reveals his trapped position in these words:

> How am I, an a-temporal being imprisoned in time and space, to escape from my imprisonment, when I know that outside space and time lies Nothing, and that I, in the ultimate depths of my reality, am Nothing also?[2]

Artistic expression is given to man's hopelessness by Francis Bacon, one of Britain's leading painters. His major theme is the sheer horror of existence. His canvases are full of screaming people, prison cages, and gory slabs of beef. From his own admission,

Bacon paints man "in the hell of his situation." The artist himself is addicted to gambling and did his finest work in a drunken state. Desperation is written all over his life and work. Yet he illustrates the truth of the Scriptures, without Christ, without hope.

William Golding captures an aspect of this mood in *Lord of the Flies*. A group of plane-wrecked British schoolboys stranded on an island (boat-shaped to symbolize the journey of life) completely shatters the myth of human innocence. We all live east of Eden. The fig leaves of man's pretensions to uprightness and nobility are torn away. In the mirror of this play we see our evil and our guilt, and the sight of it merely augments the problem.

Modern man has experienced a rude awakening. There is a recognition of something terribly wrong. These testimonies are not the opinions of pathological pessimists. These spokesmen are intellectual leaders of our culture. Today's prophets are secular.

The factors causing the death of hope are not at all mysterious. The illness began the day man placed all his confidence in himself. Since that day he has been living on borrowed capital, and today his resources are almost completely exhausted. Two factors are sufficient to explain his current bankruptcy:

The Intrinsic Logic of His Position

The dilemma of modern humanism can be explained with terrifying simplicity. Matter plus time plus chance equals zero! If man is the illegitimate offspring of a thoughtless parent order, the mockery of fortuitous chance, his significance is nil. There is no conceivable way to construct a meangingful dwelling for man upon the uncongenial foundations of chaos and accident. Modern man has simply come to realize the logical

implications of his foolish autonomy and is beginning
to pay the price. Sartre was right, this fact *ought* to
give him nausea. The further man moves toward
epistemological self-consciousness as a non-Christian,
the closer he will come to nihilism and despair. The
more consistent, the less happy. The equation of
naturalism is simple, but devastating.

Man's Inhumanity to Man

Alfred Lord Tennyson saw man moving forward
and upward, working out the beast, and letting ape
and tiger die. But that was the nineteenth century. The
beast in man refused to die. Instead, he grew larger.
The optimistic hope for the educated, moral man of
tomorrow never crystallized. "The heart is deceitful
above all things, and desperately wicked" (Jer 17:9).
Whereas it was once ridiculed, the doctrine of original sin is again respected as an essential insight into
human nature. Before any humanistic utopia can be
reached, a transformation in the human factor must
be made. A possibility of this exists in the new being
of the gospel, but little hope remains outside its
boundaries. Man is at the end of his tether. The facts
of history discourage him, and the logic of naturalism
crushes him. A cry goes up to heaven, "How long?"

The death *of* hope leads directly to the hope *for*
death. For man still cherishing his ideals, death is an
enemy. But to him whose life is pointless, death is a
sweet savior. Hemingway embraced it as his messiah.
Camus named suicide as the only truly serious philosophical problem. Death, without further possibility
of good or evil, is preferable to life without hope. The
set of choices is admittedly a bleak one, but it is all
the choice the non-Christian has left. Preoccupation
with death is a distinguishing mark of our time. The

"death of God" controversy ought to be set in its
proper context. Our era at the same time glorifies
and hates death. Its prominence in Freud, Heidegger,
Kafka and Bacon is a sure sign of a collapsing culture. A philosophy of life which does not make its
terms with death cannot hope to survive. For most
people it is a topic as distasteful to discuss as it is
impossible to evade. Yet it is the source of the deepest
anguish in the human breast. Death, a fall into a
bottomless void, strikes fear to the heart. Modern
man is fast approaching the place where he hates life
and fears death. His only hope lies with Him who can
extract the sting from death, and grant a more abundant life.

The rising curve of contemporary secularism has
almost reached the point of complete cynicism. From
this point the line may turn in a parabola to a new
basis for hope, either in a new mysticism grounded
in the creative imagination (the existential way), or
back to the historical Christian faith, on which foundation a durable cultural edifice could be constructed.
Victor Hugo wrote, "There is nothing so powerful in
all the world as an idea whose time has come." It is
surely the time for a vigorous restatement of the
Christian faith in the firm confidence that its restora-
tion to the basis of our culture would lead our nation
to health and vigor again.

The radical unmasking required today cannot be
done by Evangelicals who are culturally barren, however. Where there is no serious interest in literature
and the arts, there can be no effective communication
of the gospel to our contemporaries at large. Each
Christian does not need to be a literary critic himself,
but his ears ought to be attuned to the sound of his
world; and the Christian community should be a place

in which these interests are encouraged, not shunned. In general, Christians are culturally uninformed, much like the man who, when asked if he had purchased the new *Random House Dictionary of the English Language,* replied, "I'm waiting for the film version." Until we stop relying on instant culture, the abbreviated book and the weekly digest, the task of effective evangelism will not get done. Cultural and spiritual growth *are* related. The enlarged capacity created by an appetite for a wider spectrum of cultural interest will increase our intake ability for spiritual truth too.

It is sadly ironical that those best acquainted with our culture seldom have answers to its dilemmas, while those with the answer hide their treasure behind barricades of ignorance. The Christian life ought to exhibit richness, not poverty. Only thus can we hope to penetrate the defenses of those who perish through want of a vision. Our generation will not be impressed with the language of Zion, the mouthing of empty clichés. If we hope to change our culture, we will have to change our lives and take the gospel seriously. A clear demonstration of the existence of God is called for in every sector of life and culture. It is lacking in so much of contemporary American churchianity.

4

STAMP OUT REALITY!

THE ESCAPE ROUTE from despair is a flight from reason. The older humanist was rational in methodology and naturalistic in premises. But the new humanist, instead of recognizing his *naturalism* to be the root of the whole problem, turns away from rationality itself. The explanation is simple: the only way to avoid the impasse of naturalism without bowing to God is to slay the dragon, reason. For irrationality is preferable in nonchristian thought to either logical despair or rational theism. Having lost their confidence in the world of reality, the artist, playwright, poet and theologian have retreated into the area of nonrational, subjective, personal experience. "Faith" becomes the magical wand which transforms despair, based on logical considerations, into hope based on the creative imagination. Metaphysical despair is the unavoidable axiom of a godless philosophy. Reality becomes an enormous steel trap, an inhuman prison, mocking man's dreams and aspirations. The revolt against reason, the characteristic mental attitude of our age, has religious roots and is directed against the *Logos,* Jesus Christ, who created all things by the word of His power (Jn 1:3; Heb 1:3). It is the denial of God's structure in order to replace it with a man-centered structure.

The popularity of Albert Camus among the beatnik, the New Left, and the avant garde artistic movements is understandable in the light of the passion to smash reason. The late Algerian playwright had a brilliant sense of the tragic in life. He bares his heart in *The Plague, The Outsider,* and *The Myth of Sisyphus.* Life is futile and purposeless. His answer is absurd joy in the face of unspeakable suffering and death, a pathetic irrational wish that reality would be different than it appears in his godless system. Jean Paul Sartre travels the same path. The two great ontological human experiences are anxiety and nausea. They reveal the absurdity at the base of all existence. But Sartre cannot live consistently with his philosophy. He can find meaning only by going against it. He was quoted as saying, "Man is absurd, but he must grimly act *as if* he were not." In other words, the non-Christian must live in pretense, against the logic of his own position. Atheists exist like Sartre, but consistent ones do not. Atheism is more on the lip than in the life. A world truly absurd contains nothing but chaos. It is without values, rationality, hope. Not the grimmest existentialist lives in a world like this.

For over a century the Huxley family has been famous for its naturalistic humanism. Aldous Huxley began his career as a skeptic of all absolute values. But in his closing years in Southern California, he evolved a philosophy of hope based on a mescalin drug experience. When "tuned in," Huxley received "a mystic awareness of the richness of bare being," a "goodness encompassing good and bad." Although Huxley thought his life was crowned by this mystic discovery, his shift from rationality to this nonrational drug mysticism actually indicated the bankruptcy of naturalism in the Huxley family. The delight his brother Julian finds in Teilhard de Chardin, the mystical Catholic Darwinian, is evidence of the same flight from reason. Humanism is too bad to be true. All the labor expended in human causes seems rather futile where no goal is in view. How can one justify life in a meaningless universe? The nonchristian answer is to move up into its own version of the "upper story," the realm of dream and illusion, where perchance hope can be recovered through a mystical leap of faith. Carl F. H. Henry was fully justified in writing:

> The whole frame of reference within which modern man seeks the meaning of life and the solution of his persistent problems, displays its inadequacies in test after test.[1]

The short circuit to hopelessness brought on by the logic of naturalism is provided by a mystical, and essentially religious, leap of faith. Julian Huxley saw the need for a religion without revelation. That is, a religion that would give cozy warmth of undefined symbols without the interference of a God who actually exists. Thus Huxley himself manipulates lofty symbols like "destiny," "values," "shared responsibility" and "evolutionary goals" in order to cover up the apparent void created by his own system. Out of nothingness only nothingness can come. A logical locomotive will not stop just because someone screams. Huxley's integrity is in real doubt. Having set the train in motion, he now leaps off as the precipice approaches, and hides behind the ancient oak of mysticism. Not a very impressive end to a century of rationalism.

The movement of Western thought toward the East is apparent in all of this. The growing popularity of Zen Buddhism among the cultural avant garde in

America is due to its deliberate irrationality. In Zen, reason (*vijnana*) and the intuition (*prajna*) are always in contrast. Mystical subjectivism belongs properly to the East, not to Christianity. The Zen master Professor Suzuki correctly rebukes certain Christian mystics who erase the creature-Creator distinction, the transcendence of God over the world. For historic Christianity based on the Bible is not the home of mysticism and irrational faith. The current attempt to link up Eastern mysticism with Western theism (e.g., Altizer) is an example of pure wishful thinking. It is *Zen* which gives irrationalism its proper home, the repudiation of true meaning for aesthetics and intuition. In Zen, the individual can excuse himself from all responsibility, and withdraw into a contemplation of his navel. Man, reason and culture—all are dead.

The retreat from reason into the subjective realm can be traced on every side of our culture. An example is the new turn in Martin Heidegger's thought from his earlier analysis of the ontological significance of man's "feeling states" to his recent interest in the poet Hölderin and the prophetic meaning of poetry. The visionary grasps intuitively the shape of being and gives it expression in the poetic word, a "revelation" of being in language. Heidegger escapes from the real, palpable world in which by logic he can find no answer. By attaching himself to poetic intuition and making the poet his priest, he aspires to overcome the discomfort of a rational world. The action painting of Jackson Pollack and the chance music of John Cage fit into the same category. By a repudiation of all rational controls, both men hope to create meaningful forms by the operation of *chance,* the ultimate spring of all creativity to them. (Bacon's addiction to gambling needs to be viewed in this light.)

Similarly the sex-mysticism of Terry Southern or
Henry Miller is a desperate attempt to launch oneself
into a mystical orbit, where hopefully some answers
to life's enigmas can be encountered.

But undoubtedly the clearest example of the retreat
from reason is found at the *psychedelicatessen*. If the
desire is to manipulate contentless symbols which give
the appearance of communication without challenging
naturalism, then LSD and its family of hallucogenic
drugs is without question the sacrament of the movement. For it enables the devotee to move onto the
"upper story" with incredible ease. Drugs create a
heightened self-awareness, and a mystical sensation of
being united with nature. All the senses are expanded
and jumbled. Color can be tasted and sound smelled.
The aim is to *disorient* the mind so that the individual
can detach himself from the real world and commune
with the beyond. Salvation is a coin-operated electric
Kool-Aid machine! The drug can propel you into
Nirvana *now;* so why wait? The conversion of Timothy
Leary to Hinduism is hardly surprising. Religion in the
East is beyond intellect and conviction. It is a world
of nondiscrimination and nondifferentiation. The great
irony in the Eastward movement of the West is the
belief that this trend is a *forward* step. Millennia
ago men in the East lost all hope for rational answers
and opted for mystical pantheism, a decision which
produced the immobile giants of Eastern culture. At
the same time the decision destroyed the basis for
initiative, thrift, purpose and vitality.

The drug experiment is a part of the "exploration
of inner space," the attempt to locate *within* the soul
a clue to meaning which has not been discovered
outside it. On the evolutionary view that religions are
the product of human development rather than its

explanation, psychedelic drugs can be useful in re-creating the myths of ancient people in order to use them as a medicine for modern psychoses. Simply by going on a trip, a person can enjoy a conversion like St. Paul's, according to Professor Pahnke. Possibly enough LSD might even produce a resurrection appearance! Modern man worships at the shrine of the unconscious and looks to biochemistry for a savior. It is however a great *delusion*. LSD will convince a person of powers he does *not* have, and answers he does *not* possess. In real life, the Captain Marvel who leaps from the window of a skyscraper is dead. The drug taker has two choices: a one-way ticket to an asylum, or a shelf in the deep freeze for spiritual dropouts. Neither a bad trip nor a good trip can secure what a man really needs, namely, a Creator and Saviour who is really *there*. The drug movement is a desperate attempt to find meaning in a world where none exists apart from Jesus Christ. It is a pure escape from life which has become unbearable. LSD only gives the illusion of adding to one's stock of answers. The salvation that cannot save a sober man is unlikely to save an intoxicated one. Leary's dictum — "It becomes necessary to go out of our minds in order to use our heads"—is a counsel of despair, a salvation by self-destruction. Only the abnormal can find this blessedness. It is only the gospel which speaks to the *total* man today.

The resemblance of the LSD solution to the mentality of the upper-story theology cannot have escaped notice. Each is moving away from a rational answer toward a nonrational existential religious experience without content. Salvation is reached through a "final experience." In theology, the drugs may be employed in order to speed up the manipulation of symbols, as in recent experiments at Boston University, where divinity students tuned in to a deeper meditation on Good Friday with the aid of the "sacrament." But there are other ways of turning on. The dramatic rise of occurrences of tongue-speaking fits into this picture too. Release from anxiety can be obtained by letting the mind go free to the accompaniment of soft babblings from the throat. The appearance of the "gift" at Notre Dame, and its results, a greater love for the mass and the rosary ought to alert thoughtful Protestants to the extreme dangers implicit in the movement, simply because of its wider context, the widespread retreat from all rational controls. Biblical Christianity is rooted in historical (1 Co 15:14) and rational truth (1 Jn 4:3). Drugs only mess up the genuine believer, because his worship is based on objective truth, not dreams or myths. A "trip" is as likely to open the individual to demonic invasion as it is to edify him.

The real threat of the retreat from reason in whatever form it may take is its implications for world religion and world government, two treasured goals of international liberalism. The new emphasis on mystic feelings has softened our generation up for the imprinting of whatever world view the rulers of tomorrow may wish to impose. The perfect instrument is now ready for the ultimate ruler in an omnicompetent and omnipotent state to herd the human population into the barns of his choosing. The current openness of leading Marxist intellectuals to dialogue with Christians stems less from a true softening on their part than from a realization that the new theology in Protestant circles contains nothing that Communism needs to fear. For a religion rooted in the Social Gospel, which thinks of man primarily in terms of

mass social and political forces, is an ally, rather than
an enemy, of Marxism. A grand political-religious col-
lusion of the kind pictured in Revelation 13 and 17
is certainly within the realm of possibility in the near
future. In George Orwell's *1984,* all history was a
palimpsest, scraped clean and reinscribed exactly
as often as was necessary. Whenever the interpretation of history and fact becomes an arbitrary
subjective decision, mankind is subjected to a
totalitarian ideology. History becomes the servant
in the hands of the regime, and a tool of social en-
gineering. It spells the death of the individual and the
culture. But this is precisely the direction in which
we are presently moving, away from reason and history, into the horrors of subjective existentialism. The
Nazi movement has given the world a horrible object
lesson when a world view is detached from historical
fact. The myths become autonomous and destructive.
The Christian faith is rooted in the *real.* It bases its
claims on historical events. It is altogether opposed to
the contemporary intellectual climate.

5

THE BREAKING POINT

ROMANTICISM is the procedure of giving an optimistic
answer to the human dilemma without a sufficient
base for so doing. From the Christian point of view,
the death of hope and romanticism was a beneficial
thing. Romanticism is an enemy of the gospel because
it lulls people into a false security. The avant garde
artist may be unpleasant, but he is at least rather
honest. Mantovani's music is more anti-christian than
Samuel Beckett's plays simply because it drugs the
non-Christian into peaceful slumber when he ought to
be awakened to the existence of a real problem—his
life and destiny. A sensitive believer can only feel deep
agony in his heart in the realization that the last
pocket of romanticism to die is right inside the
bourgeois church itself. Almost unconsciously, religious people regard the middle-class nonchristian
resident of a lily-white suburb as nicer, more polite
and thrifty, cleaner and kinder. But according to the
biblical faith, it is the *godly,* not the *good,* who will
be saved (Gal 2:16). Moralism without the Christian
base is a one-way ticket to hell. American Sunday
school humanism is a menace to Christianity. The
gospel is theism, not moralism. The "nice behavior
equals nice times" mentality is at the root of why
we are losing our children to secularism. Romanticism

must die before the gospel can be taken seriously. Everyone has watched the late show in which the hero gets the girl, the villain is apprehended, and everybody lives happily afterward. Far from being a "Christian film," this kind of idealism is a *lie*. The great merit of the most radical novelist today is that at least he is not complacent. The death of romanticism is a *good* thing for the gospel. Our culture has moved so far toward nihilism that the two leading artists who are called humanists, Francis Bacon and Alberto Giacommetti (because they depict human subjects), actually paint so gloomy a picture of life that they would have been scorned a century ago by the humanists of that day.

There is not a single art form which does not bear the scars of the death of romanticism. As men realize the logical implications of their unbelief they move gradually and irresistibly toward the breaking point, steadily losing a grip on their humanity, and finding themselves unable to operate in the real world. In philosophy, for example, serious grappling with ultimate questions of life and death has almost vanished, replaced by word games and language analysis. With the loss of absolutes since Hegel, in which the distinction between true and false, right and wrong, breaks down, the philosopher is virtually out of a job. Or, one need only trace the sad history of art in the past hundred years, from impressionism to cubism, to dada, to surrealism, to pop, to op, to psychedelic art. The exercise can bring sadness to the person who treasured the culture which the Reformation produced. In the same manner there is more significance in the scrapings of John Cage and Karlheinz Stockhausen than merely the invention of electric oscillators. Something has died in music—perhaps music itself. Bach wrote to the glory of Jesus. Cage writes out of homage to chance. That the products should differ should scarcely surprise us. Certainly the phenomenon of the absurd, in theater, in poetry, in novel, and in the happenings, ought to awaken us all to the desperate plight of modern man.

The longer men dwell in the prison of naturalism, the closer the parallels become between the freeman and the inmate of a real penitentiary. Samuel Beckett was quite nervous before the performance of his play *Waiting for Godot* at San Quentin prison before an audience of some 1,400 prisoners. He asked himself how they would receive the sophisticated and symbolic play. They loved it! For the simple reason that the world Beckett describes, in which every non-Christian lives, is a prison, and the inmates recognized it at once. The absurd world of Samuel Beckett is not a whit more attractive than the gray existence of a penal institution. The immediate and distant horizons are bleak. There is nothing to compensate for the effort of living. The individual is a number, merged into the herd, without independent value or significance. Upon release, he is helpless to fend for himself because personal convictions have rotted away. There are no foundations left to build upon.

Each culture and every individual exists, somewhere on the line of despair and has an individual breaking point. With the advance of the nonchristian ethos in Western civilization there will be increasing consistency in the application to all areas of life of the naturalistic premises. The more consistent a person is in putting the nonchristian position into practice, the more evident it will become to him and others what it really means to be a non-Christian. Man is in the process of self-destruction in the twentieth century. The speed at which he reaches his breaking point is determined by the degree of epistemological self-awareness he exhibits. He must learn to live honestly without God and Christ, without continuing to borrow from the capital of divine revelation and redemption. Neo-paganism in the post-Christian era must inevitably become a lot poorer before it will fabricate riches of its own. Seldom has this fact been better expressed than by Rushdoony:

> Wherever man asserts his independence of God, saying in effect, that, while he will deny God, he will not deny life, nor its relationships, values, society, its sciences and art, he is involved in contradiction. It is an impossibility for man to deny God and still to have law and order, justice, science, anything, apart from God. The more man and society depart from God, the more they depart from all reality, the more they are caught in the net of self-contradiction and self-frustration, the more they are involved in the will to destruction and the love of death (Prov. 8:36). For man to turn his back on God, therefore, is to turn towards death; it involves ultimately the renunciation of every aspect of life.
>
> To deny God, man must ultimately deny that there is any law, or reality. The full implications of this were seen in the last century by two profound thinkers, one a Christian, the other a non-Christian. Nietzsche recognized fully that every atheist is an unwilling believer to the extent that he has any element of justice or order in his life, to the very extent that he is even alive and enjoys life. In his earlier writings, Nietzsche first attempted the creation of another set of standards and values, affirming life for a time, until he concluded that he could not affirm life itself, nor give it any meaning, any value, apart from God. Thus Nietzsche's ultimate counsel was suicide; only then, can we truly deny God, and,

in his own life, this brilliant thinker, one of the
clearest in his description of modern Christianity
and the contemporary issue, did in effect commit a
kind of psychic suicide. The same concept was
powerfully developed by Dostoyevsky, particularly in
The Possessed, or, more literally, the Demon Possessed. Kirilov, a thoroughly Nietzschean character,
is very much concerned with denying God, asserting
that he himself is God, and that man does not need
God. But at every point, Kirilov finds that no standard or structure in reality can be affirmed without
ultimately asserting God, that no value can be as-
serted without being ultimately derived from the
triune God. As a result, Kirilov committed suicide
as the only apparently practical way of denying God
and affirming himself, for to be alive was to affirm
this ontological deity in some fashion.[1]

There is at the present time, then, a radical disintegration of the nonchristian man as he reaps the
harvest produced by the seed he has sown. After many
years the crop is approaching full maturity, and the
ingathering is proving a most unpleasant time. He
has laid up treasures on the earth, the sphere of his
ultimate values, the place of his only reward and en-
joyment. His values are dead on the vine, being merely
the dictates of social and personal convenience. The
ethic of evolution, the survival of the fittest, has yet
to take its full toll. The world has still to see the full
maturing of de Sade's "natural behaviour" based on
the principle of "what is, is right." The simple equation—matter plus time plus chance—has yet to yield
its full horror.

However, a man does not exist who does not fall
short of total consistency. Each non-Christian holds to
a mixed world view. It is impossible to live inside his
system logically, so he borrows liberally from gospel

capital, on his own terms, of course. He loves what the gospel can give him (rationality, significance, pardon, identity), but will not part with his autonomy and hence must steal from the Christian system to survive. The more consistent he is with himself, the closer he draws to the breaking point. Having first discarded God, he tends to jettison anything which smacks of association with God, which, as he finds in the end, is everything worth having. Therefore, he stalls his engine on the line of despair in the attempt to avoid either distasteful termination, salvation under God or despair in a naturalistic prison house. Every non-Christian inhabits a halfway house somewhere in his experience. Hugh Hefner, the ingenious juggler of American symbols, is noted for his advocacy of unlimited sexual license. However, in a recent interview, Hefner admitted his distaste for a woman who actually put his philosophy into effect. Furthermore, when asked whether he would encourage his daughter to be promiscuous, he admitted his intellectual schizophrenia: "Intellectually I may think in a certain way; practically I may act in another way. I am and I remain a combination of incoherences that I uselessly try to reject." Hefner does not admit the logic of his position because he is unwilling to face a world with the philosophy he espouses! At least in his lover and his daughter he retains a sector of sanity and morality. But it is not to his credit. It only proves the basic dishonesty of the nonchristian position.

It has been observed in the life of a prison, that whereas a prisoner may regard no private property outside the prison sacred, very often he would under no circumstances steal from a fellow prisoner. Though he may profess a world without moral absolutes, he would on no condition squeal on a fellow prisoner. In every man there are moral motions which he can no more eradicate than fly. These are rather to his condemnation than to his credit, but they do expose the point of contact for the glorious gospel of Christ. The good news calls man back to the living God, the fountain of all rationality, love, significance, morality and freedom. It urges him to forsake his rebellion which only yields him irrationalty, absurdity, silence and despair, and to accept the Christian set of presuppositions within which life is possible. There is a danger implicit here. If you take away man's lie, you may be taking away his hope. So the Christian witness needs to act gently and in love, lest the person he seeks to win should bolt to the point of total breakdown. Unmasking the natural man is the dark side of apologetics, but a needful part. The mask must first come off if man is to see himself as he is.

The cultural point of contact for the gospel lies deep within man himself, as one created in the image of God. The inner contradiction needs to be sought out and located, so that the balm of Gilead may be applied. A person can profess disbelief in gravity, but living consistently with that profession is quite another matter. There are more atheists in lip than there are in life. In his day Jonathan Edwards sought to destroy false happiness by presenting the reality of hell and judgment. We must seek to destroy that spurious security too by whatever tool at our disposal. Starting where man is, it is our duty to inform him of his inconsistency, and at the same time both nudge him to the logic of his own position and urge him to the logic of ours. The tin roof of his hastily constructed shack must be ripped off so that the harsh elements of the real world might awaken him to his folly and stimulate him to seek Jesus Christ.

6

OUR MONOLITHIC CULTURE

TRADITIONALLY AND OFFICIALLY American is *pluralistic* in religion. Diverse convictions are held honorably and freely throughout the land, and no sect is allowed an establishment over the rest. The common bond which held the original states together was Christian culture, but each region was to practice her version without interference from the federal power. The intent of the first amendment to the American Constitution was not the creation of a secular state, but the imposing of a check on the central government from coercing the states in this matter. At the present time, however, because of the decline of Christian faith and the effectiveness of mass media, America is rapidly becoming a *monolithic* culture with uniform religious characteristics. The various cult functionaries serve a general religion of humanity and the American way of life. A striking parallel with the Roman Empire is pointed up by Gibbon:

> The various modes of worship which prevailed in the Roman world were all considered by the people as equally true; by the philosopher as equally false; and by the magistrate as equally useful. And thus toleration produced not only mutual indulgence, but even religious concord.[1]

Humanism is as much a religion as Christianity, though it is not called one. It is nonetheless the religion of the land both within the churches and without. Biblical Christianity is being pushed aside from every sector of life — science, education, welfare, government, pyschology, theology — and most people proceed with scarcely a glance at it. The country at large, the polls tell us, professes a brand of religion in surprising numbers, but the people clearly believe in the *practical* irrelevance of the gospel. At a speed which is quite amazing the nation is being conditioned to a naturalistic way of thinking, the denial of all absolutes, and the relativism of all convictions. There are characteristics of the new emerging culture which no thinking person should ignore.

One of the necessary myths of a monolithic culture is the myth of neutrality. Because man is the ultimate standard by which all things are to be measured, he is expected to approach questions of values and religion with a godlike objectivity. Strong convictions are equivalent to prejudices, firm principles to a bias. Although the politician appeals to sectional interests in order to get elected to office, the last thing in the world he must do when installed is to admit any sectional interests. Though people vote for their own self-interest, their elected officials pretend to stand for the common good while practicing brazen political deals under the table. In religion the myth of neutrality is widespread. All the creeds are equally grand — none true. Leaders speak of our Protestant-Catholic-Jewish heritage as if such a hyphenated monstrosity really meant something. (If the hippies have their way, we shall soon have to attach Zen to that designation.) It is nice to have convictions, so long as you don't believe they are true! In this context a real Christian,

who believes the name of Jesus is the only name under
heaven capable of saving (Ac 4.12), is an unrecon-
structed bigot. He knows, however, with the proverb,
"The one who says he is not prejudiced is a liar," that
this neutrality is destructive and false. The proper
procedure is to have the courage of your prejudices!
Man according to the Bible is set in a particular culture and approaches reality with a religious set of
categories to which he has committed himself. The
man who pretends a lofty neutrality above the mass
of men is more vulnerable to human sins than the
person who admits his perspective and respects the
viewpoints of others. The new citizen, friendly to all
convictions, but attached to none, is a menace. The
trend can only issue in the destruction of all values.

A monolithic culture tends to level values to the
lowest common denominator to avoid unpleasant divi-
sion and strife among men. Firm convictions are a
threat because they divide men who share them from
those who do not. Hence in a monolithic culture only
the beliefs held in common are absolute. If prayer in
the state school offends 4 per cent of the pupils, none
should engage in it. If 10 per cent of the students
prefer homosexual to heterosexual relations, equal
time must be given to teaching both sides. The pupils
learn that "values" are important for life, but also
that no way exists for knowing which values. Many
are convinced that Albert Schweitzer's ideas were
higher than Himmler's; but since both were carried
out sincerely, it is difficult to explain the basis for
such a preference. The only really sacred thing in a
monolithic culture is social harmony. Convictions
which divide men ought to be kept private and not be
allowed to intrude in the public sector. This virtual
"erosion of the mind," an avalanche of facts without

a hermeneutic, leads directly to the disintegration of a culture. The loss of identity, the incapacity for action, the frustrated violence, the painful rootlessness of our day—all trace back to the relativism of humanism. We hear of antireligious conditioning in the Soviet schools, and find security in the costly myth that our own schools are neutral. Yet, it is almost the expected thing for a Christian coming to the university to find his beliefs attacked unmercifully by zealous faculty members who see it as their messianic task to wipe his mind clean of all inherited ideas and implant within it the one conviction, that there are no absolutes. Conviction beyond that is a crime. Bland humanism is the key to advancement. The anesthesia of culture the goal. Relativism is moral and intellectual atrophy. It results in the destruction of genuine morality (for inhumanity is a way of life too), and of freedom (for human "rights" become arbitrarily defined by the divine state). It is the direct antithesis of the gospel which claims universal validity and application to all men.

The faith of our monolithic culture which is emerging is the religion of humanity. The happiness of man is the single tenet, and whatever is human is sacred. The way of salvation is through the restructuring of the social environment and results in the satisfaction of the desires of all men. To achieve the goal of universal happiness, however, it is first necessary to remove all discriminatory legislation and prohibitions. Revolution and freedom are the key words. A law which restricts the freedom of some groups causes pain to them and is unfairly discriminatory. The "civil rights" movement for the homosexual is already in full swing thanks to the Mattachine Society, the Wofendon Report, and the ecumenical Council for Religion and the Homosexual. The cry for freedom is a cry for anarchy, the destruction of all revealed law and its replacement by a fluid set of humanly appointed rules. *Vox populi* equals *vox dei*. Man is holy. The most lurid display of perversion and sadism is culturally significant. Whatever is, is right. At last the philosophy of Marquis de Sade may win the day.

The religion of humanity forbids any absolutes. Doctrinal convictions discriminate against unbelievers. Taking the gospel to the Jews, for example, is an anti-Semitic act because it introduces an antithesis into society. The refusal to pray with a Unitarian minister is interpreted as sheer bigotry in the context of the religion of humanity, for which the only inviolable credo is "In Man We Trust."

In order to deal effectively with this generation for Christ, it is imperative to detect the shape of this humanistic culture. Let us select three areas in which the new mentality is deeply ingrained already: government, education and science.

In the biblical understanding, the state is a necessary evil. There is no sociological form in a fallen world without force. The state is an emergency measure instituted by God to suppress evil which constantly threatens to overwhelm the world. The eras of greatest misery to the human race are those in which governmental power is broken altogether. However, the Bible does not think of the state *messianically* either. It too requires restraint to keep it from becoming an antichrist. The framers of the American Constitution were aware of human nature, and provided for checks and balances in the system, whereby the power would be widely distributed and not accumulate in the hands of a few. The humanistic view of the state is totally different. It is a human invention, designed to lead mankind to paradise on earth. If the citizens would hand over their incomes, their lands, and their resources to the beneficent state, the latter would reward them bountifully. Socialism or collectivism is the political system of humanism.. The state is the domestic and inter-national savior. "From each according to his ability, to each according to his need." The divine state provides cradle-to-the-grave security, and asks only the total ownership of country and people. From the biblical viewpoint, however, blind confidence in the omnicompetent state is disastrous. Political charity is no charity at all! The concentration of power in the hands of a few men can only work us ill. Government is not a Santa Claus. It is not the source of any of the goods it grandly bestows on the people. Everything it gives to the people it has first taken from the people. The current move toward collectivism in America is based on a humanistic view of man, his nature and problems, and we may all live to regret it.

Education has become the property of the state in America, and increasingly of the federal power. In the Bible, education is the duty of the *home*. Believing parents are admonished to rear their children as a sacred trust from God and in His fear and worship (Deu 6:7; Pr 22:6; Eph 6:4). It is their fundamental covenantal duty. In the early years of American history, education was handled locally, in line with the ideals of parents and community. But with the rise to prominence of the public schools, responsibility for the child's education shifted from parent to state. The children effectively became the property of the state, under its influence and jurisdiction, for a large part of the week, and for the formative years of their lives. It then became the aim of liberal humanism to use education in the conditioning of society into a mono-

lithic culture. The primary aim of education was to be
the social adjustment of children into a group-oriented
mentality. This involved the elimination from the cur-
riculum of beliefs and values not universally held. The
education became child-centered, not content-centered,
and stressed self-development rather than his learning
of the wisdom of the past. Statist education is becoming a major threat to the church in America. As it
becomes increasingly secularist and humanistic, Christian parents will come to realize how impossible it is
to raise their children in the Christian faith while
throwing them to the wolves in their education. Education may prove to be the point at which the drift
toward collectivism is stopped. The striking increase
in Christian schools across the country may arrest the
growth of statism and the monolithic culture.

Science means one thing to the expert practitioners
in various fields, and quite another to the general public which is subject to the propaganda of scientism.
Science is a sacred cow, and one of its most persistent
myths in the twentieth century is the nebulous concept, "evolution." Christians are constantly asked
whether they "believe" it, as if the word conveyed
anything specific. It is always easier to detect the
myths of other people than to discern one's own. The
myth of evolution is so entwined in the current world
view that its absurdities are seldom even noticed. It
ought to be apparent to the casual observer of the
history of science since Darwin, that the theory he
propounded, far from becoming better established, has
become shakier with every passing year. If you ignore
for a moment the brainwashing of magazines with a
Time-Life mentality, and listen to the experts in the
various fields, you would soon realize that the data on
which this grand hypothesis depends are slender in-

deed, and capable of a dozen different constructions. The *fact* is that the basic requirement, the spontaneous origin of life, has never been observed or demonstrated, and in the light of probabilities and the laws of thermodynamics, is a most unlikely hypothesis. The reason evolution is believed and taught as fact is not due to the evidence for it, but rather due to the *need* for it. Any "natural miracle" (that inert matter is creative) is preferable to a humanist over a "supernatural miracle" (that God is the Creator). The state schools do everything they can to promote the myth because it is essential to the religion of humanity. Man cannot be autonomous if there exists a transcendent God with a divine law. Such a God must die. Evolution is accepted because it shuts Him out, and leaves man free. But what an awful freedom! The freedom to know nothing, to be nothing, to believe nothing. The words of Paul have never been more fitting in the history of the world than now: "Professing themselves to be wise, they became fools" (Ro 1:22).

The only absolute in our monolithic culture is that there are no absolutes; the only belief that all beliefs are relative. One thing is right—that which seems good in your own eyes; and one thing holy—humanity. The philosophical significance of pornography in our day is the concerted attempt to use it in the breakup of all standards. By debauchery of every kind it is hoped to transcend all antithesis and achieve "freedom." By a return to chaos, from whence all has sprung, salvation is being sought. God is dead. Only man and his caretaker state remain. All differentiation in truth and morals is swallowed up. A mystical pantheism is all that remains; all the colors shade into one another. Man is lost in hopelessness. His is the integration into the void.

7

VALIDATING THE GOSPEL

IN THE WAKE of a radical unmasking, the sun of righteousness appears all the brighter in its splendor. But it is insufficient merely to show another position is faulty and untrue unless it can also be shown that the gospel itself is well founded. It is not enough that the Christian faith should be pragmatically true or personally rewarding unless its substance can stand the test of rigorous investigation. Validation is the task of Christian evidences, an important subsection of apologetics. Myths and fables are immune to historical research and analysis, but the Christian message is open to examination. Apologetics takes the *incarnation* just as seriously as theology does. Both are centered in Christ. His advent and ministry provide both the redemptive content and the epistemological grounding of our faith. The Christian faith is an intelligent faith. Apologetics' concern is to provide evidence that the ground on which the structure rests is firm.

Ideally our approach to the question of validation should arise from biblical data. Upon examination it appears that Scripture provides a broad hint concerning the shape of our defense of the faith. In both Old and New Testaments the same pattern emerges: that divine revelation is accompanied by supernatural indicia, namely, prophecy (supernatural knowledge) and miracle (supernatural power). These accompany the acts of God and His prophetic words.

In the Old Testament the true prophet may be identified by the test of whether what he predicts actually comes to pass (Deu 18:21-22). One of the distinguishing characteristics of the living God over against the false gods was His capacity to announce the future beforehand (Is 41:21-24; 42:9; 45:21 46:11). His ability through His spokesmen to transcend the alphabet of human knowledge provided objective proof of His sovereignty over history.

In the New Testament Jesus repeatedly predicts His crucifixion and its outcome in the resurrection. This was to be the ultimate sign with which He would provide men (Jn 2:18-21). At the resurrection two miracles meet: His predictions are fulfilled (Mk 8:31), and God's power is demonstrated (Ro 1:4).

In the Old Testament the existence of God is established by an appeal to historical evidence. Moses was worried that Israel would not listen to his words from God. To counteract the incredulity of the people, Moses was given the gift of miracle-working (Ex 4:1 ff.). After the mighty hand of God had been seen in the miraculous timing of the Red Sea miracle, Israel believed anew in the Lord's power (Ex 14:30-31). At a later date God asked Moses: "How long will they not believe in me, [in spite of] all the signs which I have wrought among them?" (Num 14:11, ASV). Rahab came to faith in the Lord when she encountered good and sufficient evidence for the reality of Israel's God (Jos 2:8-11). Gideon's doubts were quieted by divine signs capable of overcoming his hesitation to act (Judg 6:13, 17, 37, 40). On Mount Carmel the prophet Elijah called for a great confrontation with the prophets of Baal (1 Ki 18). "The God who answereth by fire, let him be God" (v. 24.) In reply to Elijah's faith the Lord acted, and in the miracle demonstrated His existence and power for all the people.

In the New Testament, Jesus Christ appears on the scene making tremendous claims for Himself. His lofty teachings concerning His own deity were authenticated by the performance of miraculous signs. The gospel of Mark is replete with examples of the evidential value of miracles (Mk 1:28, 45; 2:10; 5:19, 42-43; 6:2, 14; 7:37; 8:18-21, etc.). The gospel of John is preeminently the gospel of signs. After the miracle at Cana, His disciples believed on Him (2:11). Upon the healing of his son, the official believed in Jesus (4:53). "The same works that I do bear witness of me that the Father hath sent me" (5:36). When the people saw the miracle of feeding the five thousand, they recognized Jesus to be the Prophet, the Messianic King (6:14-15). Jesus performed so many signs that the people had a dilemma: "When the Christ shall come, will he do more signs than those which this man hath done?" (7:31, ASV). The raising of Lazarus from the dead caused many to believe on Jesus (11:45), and goes far to explain why so large a crowd gathered at His triumphal entry (12:9-12, 18). "If I had not done among them the works which none other man did, they had not had sin: but now have they both seen and hated both me and my Father" (15:24). Thomas brings the gospel to its theological finale in his confession to Jesus, "My Lord and my God!" (20:28). But he came to this conviction after receiving objective proof that Jesus had indeed risen as the disciples had said. "Many other signs therefore did Jesus in the presence of the disciples, which are not written in this book: but these are written, that ye may believe that Jesus is the Christ, the Son of God; and that believing ye may have life in his name" (20:30-31, ASV).

The miracles of Christ provided men with a powerful incentive to trust Him: "Even though you do not believe *me*, believe the *works*, that you may know and understand that the Father is in me" (Jn 10:38). In another situation Jesus chided the cities of Chorazin and Bethsaida for not believing on the basis of good and sufficient evidences: "For if the mighty works done in you had been done in Tyre and Sidon, they would have repented long ago in sackcloth and ashes" (Mt 11:21). Conversely, when John the Baptist was perplexed about the identity of Jesus, his attention was drawn to the miracles Jesus performed as evidence of the dawning of the Messianic age: "Go and tell John the things which ye have seen and heard" (LK 7:22). In the early apostolic preaching too an appeal was made to the mighty acts of Jesus which accredited His divinity (Ac 2:22; 10:38). In like vein Paul told King Agrippa that he had no excuse for his agnosticism: "For I am persuaded that none of these things are hidden from him; for this thing was not done in a corner" (Ac 26:26). Confirmatory signs also accompanied the ministry of the apostles (Heb 2:4). "Truly the signs of an apostle were wrought among you in all patience, in signs, and wonders, and mighty deeds" (2 Co 12:12).

But undoubtedly the greatest stress in the New Testament is placed on the bodily resurrection of Jesus Christ as *the* supreme sign of the truth of the gospel. Jesus presented Himself alive after His suffering to the disciples with "many infallible proofs" (Ac 1:3). His resurrection was an attested fact of history (Ac

2:32; 10:41; 1 Co 15:3-11). It was the supreme demonstration of the deity of Jesus Christ (Ro 1:4). It provided mankind with an evidence of universal validity (Ac 17:31). "If Christ be not risen, then is our preaching vain, and your faith is also vain" (1 Co 15:14). We have a living hope *because* God raised up Jesus (1 Pe 1:3). The existential cart must remain *behind* the historical horse and not intrude in front.

This survey of biblical data assures us that a historical approach to Christian evidences is valid. There are doubtless other ways of proceeding, but this way enjoys clear biblical support. The primary basis of apologetics is the historical *datum* of the incarnation itself. The good news is not a fairy tale; it is grounded in objective events. Jesus has presented Himself as divine Messiah, and the resurrection has dramatically authenticated His claims. In this age of the nonrational existential experience, it is imperative to stress the fact that the gospel is about God's acting in the *empirical realm*. For the validation of the Christian claim we make our appeal to history.

It is important to pause here and consider the relation of Christian evidences to the work of the Holy Spirit. For obviously the mere existence of the Scriptures or historical evidences does not of itself create saving faith nor impart illumination automatically. An effective witness for Christ included two elements: the outer testimony to the gospel, and the inner testimony to its truth. The human side to evangelism is indispensable. "How shall they believe in him of whom they have not heard?" (Ro 10:14). This witness is to be convinced and convincing. Our evidences are a part of the total proclamation. The object of faith has substance. Yet unless the sovereign Spirit employs

our witness as His tool and creates the *capacity* for a
saving response (cf. Ac 16:14), our word will fall
upon cold hearts. The inner witness of the Holy Spirit
is essential to genuine faith (Ro 8:15; 1 Th 1:5), but
the truth He attests is nonetheless *truth*. Because we
cannot do everything does not imply we are to do
nothing. Our task is to present the data about Jesus.
Our effectiveness is of God's good pleasure (1 Co
3:6).

A typical reaction from the new theologians to this
concept of apologetics is shock that faith should in
any way be made dependent upon the uncertainty of
historical research. The Christian claim is, however,
firmly grounded in history. If God has not revealed
Himself unmistakably in human history, the incarnation was a failure because that was its intention.
Ninety percent of the alleged uncertainty is due to a
naturalistic methodology applied to the historical data,
reflecting an antisupernatural bias, rather than to any
actual obscurity in the facts. One can be a historian
without being a positivistic historian!

That the gospel rests upon an objective historical
foundation is a priceless asset in this world in which
there is a cafeteria of clues as to the meaning of the
universe. The basis on which we rest our defense of
the gospel consists of evidence open to *all* investigators.
The non-Christian has no right to disregard the gospel
because it is a matter of "faith" in the modern sense.
On the contrary, it is a matter of *fact*. The historical
foundations of the gospel, especially the resurrection
itself, comprise a powerful incentive and challenge to
our secular contemporaries to consider Christ and His
claims on their lives.

A parable will illustrate the dilemmas of nonverifiable religious assertions in contrast to the gospel. It is told by John W. Montgomery.

> A little green man eating toasted cheese sandwiches is sitting on a planet exactly two miles out of the range of the best telescope on earth. He is a figure who loves us, particularly if we eat toasted cheese sandwiches. He has a nasty habit of moving out of the range of the telescopes as they increase their range.[1]

The credibility of a religious claim rests upon its ability to verify its terms. If the data central to the message remains hidden to all investigation, suspicion arises about its existence. A religious claim without any way to test it out is as meaningless as a nuclear test-ban treaty without adequate checks. The experimental method of religious experience has grave disadvantages, as we shall see in the next chapter. If there is no way to check out the validity of the historical gospel, there are no criteria for distinguishing the Christs of Steiner, Swedenborg, and Mary Baker Eddy. The beauty of the gospel in the avalanche of competing religious claims is precisely the possibility we have of checking it out historically and factually.

The intent of Christian apologetics and evidences is not to coerce people to accept the Christian faith, but to make it possible for them to do so intelligently. The data we possess about the gospel is sufficient to make it sensible for the non-Christian to begin his search for the ultimate clue with Christianity. A display of evidences is aimed at encouraging people to put the gospel to the test and make their decision regarding it. Naturally the evidence we speak about is of a probable kind. Not the surest historical evidence for anything is equivalent to mathematical demonstration. That it is only probable does not mean it is worthless, however. For all legal and historical decisions are made upon the basis of probable judgment based on evidence. Since the whole of life proceeds on such a basis, it is not a weakness that Christian evidences should rest on it too. Human decisions are constantly made on the ground of probable evidence just because they are human. The choice of a world view does not depend on a different principle. The gospel makes a claim, and the claim can be tested by anyone who takes the trouble. Historical pessimism is nice amusement, but not a game anyone can play to the end. The beauty of the gospel consists in its openness to examination. God has revealed Himself in time-space history (Jn 1:14). Christ was a public Figure, and His resurrection a public event. The New Testament knows nothing of trans- supra- or meta-history! God acted in history, and it is in history that we seek Him.

8

THE INADEQUACY OF
EXPERIENCE ALONE

THE APPEAL to a personal experience of grace has always been a mark of evangelical Christianity. The gospel throws a direct tangent over to life itself. "The kingdom of God is . . . righteousness and peace and joy in the Holy Spirit" (Ro 14:17, ASV; cf. 15:13). Apart from an inner testimony of the Spirit, the outward witness to Christ remains a dead letter. However, ours is a day when the witness of the Spirit is radically distorted, changed into an escape from the essential historical and dogmatic *content* of the gospel. Perverted in this way, the appeal to subjective validation can completely blunt the cutting edge of Christian apologetics. In an era preoccupied with man's feeling states, the Christian needs to be watchful that the objectivity of God's acts and words is preserved intact.

Experience alone is too flimsy a base on which to rest the Christian system. The mere fact that a psychological event has taken place in one's brain cannot establish the truthfulness of the gospel or the metaphysical assertions of the biblical world view. Religious sensation by itself can only prove itself. The assertion "God exists" simply does not follow from the assertion "I had an experience of God." A psychological

datum cannot automatically lead to a metaphysical
discovery. However unique an experience may be, it
is capable of a number of radically differing inter-
pretations. It may be only an encounter with one's
own subconscious. Those who place all their emphasis
on a subjective validating process for apologetics
eventually reduce the content of revelation and fit it
to their taste. The central thing becomes that which
comes across to *me,* rather than what *God* has done
and spoken. The reason some theologians favor the
use of drugs to heighten religious perception is patent.
Whenever the existential cart is put before the historical horse, theology becomes a synthesis of human
superstitions, and putting LSD into the communion
wine is fair play!

An exclusive appeal to experience satisfies the humanistic tenor of our day in its focus on man rather
than God. The subject who has faith, rather than an
object of faith, receives the attention. When the religious consciousness takes the center of the stage,
doctrines recede into the background. Biblical teachings on justification, wrath, atonement, sin, trinity and
eschatology are taken with a grain of salt. For they
are only, it is said, experience-qualified concepts, aris-
ing from a particular culture, and not essential to the
Christian "faith." Israel encountered the nameless
other, the holy, and called it Yahweh. Other cultures
called it Marduk or Zeus. The unity of all religions
is found in the numinous awe felt in the presence of
the Other. Man's changing conceptions about the nature of the Other are plastic to his time and age. He
names the unknown God in the terms he knows. This
way of thinking is totally alien to Christianity. In his
diverse religions man is *not* seeking after God (Ro
3:11). The pagan worshiping his idol is not justified

by the sincerity of his "faith." Faith in itself is impotent unless it grasps the saving name of Jesus. The attempt to establish religious truth by an appeal to the data of comparative religious experience has proved a failure. Subjective responses alone cannot yield a gospel. The uniqueness of the Christian message is not found at the point of experience at all, but in the incarnation datum.

Unfortunately the evangelical Christian is more vulnerable to the new liberalism than he was to the old. The older variety was more candid in admitting its antisupernaturalism and antipathy to dogma. But the new liberalism is ingeniously subtle. It makes its appeal at the precise point where Evangelicals had been placing stress, namely, personal experience. The difference is, however, that personal experience now means the relativity of any known theological and historical content to the gospel. The new liberalism is compatible with any set of circumstances. Faith's "objectivity" turns out to be "subjectivity." God's act is not visible, not testable, not examinable, save through "faith." Instead of receiving valid data and making a decision on that basis, "faith" has been made into a cognitive magic wand, which provides an "object" whenever man exercises the faith function. No doubt these upper-story theologians wish to defend the faith against destructive criticisms, but what an enormous price to pay for that!

Under the new liberal construction it matters little whether the biblical statements are valid propositions for the church, or whether the biblical events are truly events at all. The only important thing is the experience which the *telling* of these tales induces in the receptive heart. You *can* believe the events are literal and the words true if you like, we are paternally told, but you are not bound to. The only act of God which vitally concerns *me* is the contemporary psychological event, not the far-distant historical one. Now this makes apologetics all very easy, of course. In the old days a Christian felt bound to refute the charges of the skeptic and cynic. With the new approach it hardly matters if the critic is right. Indeed, if faith be a leap, it might even increase our faith if we thought he were! And when we explain that the gospel is only true if you believe it, and on no other grounds, he will walk away smiling, for that is exactly what he thought all the time. A nasty argument has been avoided. A dialogue has taken place. Both receive prizes. Unfortunately one thing is lacking. The lost man has not been told of his need to be saved from wrath through the blood of the Lamb. An appeal to experience is *not* evangelism. Justification does not come at a certain degree of existential temperature. It is a legal declaration about the status of a man properly related to the Saviour, *whatever* he may feel like. An experience may be psychological, physiological, theological or demonic. The existential infection in modern theology has come at a disastrous time. It links hands with the secular flight from reason, and surrenders the very thing which makes Christianity strong, the veracity of God's act into history and the reliability of God's Word in Scripture.

The new theologians seek to draw fire away from their Achilles' heel by imputing unworthy motives underlying the desire for objective evidences. The attempt to construct an intelligent faith is made out to be a carnal longing for earthly security. "The greater the doubt, the greater the faith" is the incredible slogan of the new liberals. If you only had "faith," they say, then you would stop clinging to objectivity.

True sanctity is the surrendering of Bible and resurrection, and resting only in "God." While this manner of argument is excellent irrationalism, it is bad theology. Faith is a resting of the heart in the sufficiency of the evidences. The modern understanding of faith makes it virtually epistemological suicide. There is nothing to distinguish it from the crassest credulity and gullibility. Religious experiences not subject to testing procedures are used to "prove" everything from Zen to Mormonism. Historical pessimism in the roots of the gospel has nothing to do with faith. On the contrary, doubt in the reality of God's act and word is a mark of *apistia*. Faith is not believing what you know to be absurd. It is trusting what on excellent testimony appears to be true. Luther has been compared favorably with the new liberals in a way that does neither justice to him nor credit to his modern interpreters. Luther abandoned all confidence in his works-righteousness and placed his trust in the finished work of Jesus Christ for salvation. But the new theologian abandons confidence in the intellectual and historical content of the Christian message and places his trust in a subjective man-centered experience which is indistinguishable from gastric upset. There is simply no parallel there. Luther trusted an objectively true gospel, and the new liberals trust a subjectively pleasing state of mind. Luther held to faith in Christ; the new liberal to faith in faith.

Nowhere in the Bible is faith depicted as an unmotivated leap in the dark. Abraham, the father of all who believe, acted upon specific divine promises (Gen 12:3; 15:5-6 Ro 4:20-21; Heb 11:8-12). Abraham was prepared to act into the future on the *basis* of promises he was confident were divine in their origin. The Christian is expected to view the future

with hope because God raised Christ from the dead,
that is, to project a present well-founded certainty into
the future. Hebrews 11 mentions Gideon as a man of
faith too (11:32). But Gideon asked for a notable
objective proof of God's word to him (Judg 6). Are
we to believe that Abraham's faith was one of a different order than Gideon's? In the brief narrative of
Genesis we are not told the grounds on which Abraham's certainty rested, but neither does it tell us that
these grounds were lacking.

The dramatic conversion of the apostle Paul is often
made a model of the autonomy of faith in isolation
from objectifying elements. But the New Testament
prevents us from accepting such an inference. Paul's
conversion was a miracle designed to authenticate
Paul's credentials among the Lord's apostles. It included an audible voice which all the company with
him heard (Ac 9:7) and a visible light which everyone saw (22:9). A special vision to Ananias (9:10)
concerning his role in the event served to give the
whole experience a very objective cast indeed. No
doubt some new liberal would wish to object that the
light, the sound, and the vision are all Luke's objectifying elements placed in the narrative to improve
its dramatic effect for the reader, and that the "real
conversion" was inward and personal only. Such
argumentation is illicit because it adopts a certain
view of Paul's conversion a priori and then eliminates
all the evidence in the records which contradicts it!
Hardly an example of impartial historiography. But
Paul did not rest satisfied with these proofs. Immediately he began searching out proofs from the Old
Testament that Jesus was indeed the Messiah promised
(Ac 9:22; 17:2-3; 28:23). Later he visited the
Jerusalem apostles, not to talk about the weather, but

to gather further information, historical and doctrinal, essential to the gospel (Gal 1:18; 1 Co 15:3-11). The art of dangling the gospel on a subjective skyhook, while minimizing its historical grounding, is a very recent skill, and one in which a serious Christian witness hardly need develop proficiency.

The bitter fruit of this trend toward *faith in faith* is the irrelevance of all history and truth. Empty tomb, ransom, hell, judgment, infallibility, Jonah, virgin birth—all can be safely jettisoned as nonessential baggage which have little to do with religious experience. Gospel truth can just be revised to suit the consensus of the community (whatever community is suited to your taste). This whole mentality is a million miles distant from the New Testament message. It is a hermeneutic (a way of interpretation) which compares existential temperatures and ignores what Christ and the apostles *taught*. The first disciples pointed away from their experiences to the evidences that a divine Saviour had entered history, a fact amply attested by the bodily resurrection. This Lord and Saviour had instructed His disciples on the meaning of His impending death (Mk 10:45) and directed them to a deposit of God's written Word found in sacred Scripture (Lk 24:45). This claim can be inquired into and examined for its credibility and, when considered, can yield positive results.

Whereas skepticism is marked by bleak despair, the gospel of Christ yields richest joy. Experience does play an important, even indispensable, role in personal verification. But it cannot stand alone apart from other considerations. Redemption has been accomplished by the Lamb of God; now it needs to be appropriated. Men will put their trust in Christ only when we preach him in the power of the Spirit. Our part is to present

Christ as intelligently and fervently as we can, and wait for the breath of heaven. Paul warns us against a false emphasis. He says in effect: "Do not crow about spiritual resurrections, and do not boast in religious experiences, *unless* Christ has actually been raised in time-space history!" (1 Co 15:14, an expanded paraphrase). The gospel yields deep joy, and not the least of the reasons it does so is that it is *true*.

9

THE HISTORICAL DOCUMENTS

SINCE THE DEATH of the first generation of Christians, no one has been able to interview firsthand the eyewitnesses of Christ's life, death and resurrection. We are dependent upon written human testimony of the kind utilized in all historical study. But this is no cause for despair because the documents we possess are of the highest possible calibre. Pessimism concerning the trustworthiness of the New Testament is utterly unwarranted, and generally reflects ignorance of the facts. It is a matter of public *fact,* not of unreflecting *faith,* that the historical foundations underneath the Christian message are exceedingly secure.

While it is true that the original manuscripts of the four gospels have not survived, we do possess literally thousands of copies in codices and papyrus fragments, and attestation in the writings of the earliest Fathers. In order to demonstrate that this state of affairs is by no means an inherent weakness in validating the gospel, it is fitting to produce a set of comparisons from the area of ancient documents. The Roman historian Tacitus, writing early in the second century concerning events half a century earlier, is considered a first-rate historical source for the period *despite* the fact that the oldest manuscript copy of his work which remains dates from a full millennium after he wrote, and that we possess only twenty good manuscripts in all! In like manner, a full thousand years separates the writings of Caesar's *Gallic Wars* and the date of the oldest manuscript we now have. Aristotle wrote his *Poetics* three and a half centuries B.C. and the oldest manuscript dates from the eleventh century A.D., a full fourteen hundred years later! The same is true of the Greek historian Thucydides of whose work the oldest manuscript was copied thirteen hundred years after his death. In every single case cited, critical scholars do not think of dismissing the evidence because the original manuscripts have not survived. Each of the writers is considered an A-1 historical source.

In the case of the New Testament, however, the textual witness is remarkably superior. No less than four thousand Greek manuscripts have survived; and one of the best, Vaticanus, dates from a mere three hundred years after the composition of the gospels. The Chester Beatty papyri containing extensive portions of the New Testament date back to A.D. 150, while the Rylands fragment of John comes from A.D. 120. In addition we have attestation of the text in the apostolic Fathers from the turn of the first century. In short, on objective grounds we have before us documents of the greatest possible value for ascertaining the facts about Jesus Christ. The widespread distrust of the gospels does not stem from any knowledge of the facts but from anti-Christian propaganda.

Moreover, it is possible to estimate with a fair degree of certainty exactly when each of the gospels was actually written. The gospel of Mark must have been composed in its final draft about three decades after the resurrection. Early tradition consistently connects it to the apostle Peter who was martyred in the mid-sixties of the first century, and there is nothing in the gospel which gives any hint of knowledge about the catastrophe which befell Palestine in A.D. 70. The gospel of Matthew, which incorporates Markan material, was written soon after. The special Matthean sections in the gospel reflect a strongly Jewish interest which connects the author and his sources with the earliest church. Very likely the gospel of Luke was written earlier still, prior to the death of Peter and Paul, about A.D. 62. The legal details in the trial narrative of the gospel and the geographical and cultural accuracy of Acts, also written by Luke, call for an early date and presuppose close research on the part of the writer. The fact that Acts does not record the death of Paul is compelling reason to suppose this had not occurred at the time of writing. Tradition places John's gospel in the last decade of the first century. But its Jewish character and topographical accuracy imply that its author or his sources come from Palestine before the fall of Jerusalem in A.D. 70. Recent criticism of John has reversed completely the older skepticism, and come out strongly in favor of its substantial accuracy.

We possess then four outstanding documents written within a few decades of the resurrection and incorporating sources that go back much further. And all these documents claim directly or indirectly an eyewitness basis for the events they record.

There has been, however, a concerted attempt recently to get behind the written gospels and undermine their integrity from another angle. Radical "form criticism" of the gospels is the theory that the documents were not written out of an accurate historical memory, but concocted out of the creative imagination of the Christian community. By accepting "form criticism" as a legitimate literary form in Scripture,

Catholic and Protestant scholars alike have joined hand with skeptics of the past to allege myth, invention, and fraud in the very heart of our New Testament records. This fact is grievous, not because the allegations have any firm basis in reality, but because it reveals a profound theological sickness in all the churches today. The form-critical hypothesis is untenable because of a lack of any positive evidence for it. If the gospels were composed to deal with the problems of the postresurrection churches, the editing boards were singularly inept. Where in the four gospels does one find the problem of tongues discussed, or the admission of the Gentiles, or the government of the churches? Not one single problem we *know* about in the apostolic church is raised in the gospels directly. Every form-critical verdict is based on a circular argument. It is *assumed* that the gospels are sources for the history of the early church, and then it proceeds to exegete them accordingly. But, until one piece of positive evidence turns up to explain *how* the community, scattered around the then-known world, conspired together to perform so gigantic a fraud in the space of three decades, form criticism is unproven speculation. If our concern is for facts, we shall have to admit that if something has been "dissolved" in the current discussion it is form criticism itself rather than the figure of Jesus Christ.

As opposed to the biblical emphasis on history, rationalism has always tended to be antihistorical. Historical knowledge was felt to be second-rate knowledge because the degree of certainty in it was so far less than mathematical. While this mood did produce its own historians, the positivists, who sought to find this certainty in history, more often than not it produced a disengagement from history. Theologians sought to rescue the Christian faith from the fear of falsification through historical criticism by shutting it up in the subjective realm. This is the strategy adopted by Barth, Brunner, Bultmann, Tillich, Bornkamm, and a host of others. But it is utterly opposed by the New Testament insistence that God decisively revealed Himself in the empirical realm through Jesus Christ, in the midst of ordinary secular history, in the flesh and bone of history itself. The separation of saving history from ordinary history is monstrous. There is only one history. And the gospel claims that God showed Himself in that. When we ground our apologetic in historical data, we are merely doing what the apostles did before us. If the gospel cannot be sustained by historical data, it cannot be sustained at all. Faith rests upon the certainty of what God did in history (Lk 1:1-4). The current historical heresy espoused by Dilthey and Collingwood, that there can be no objective knowledge of the past, has been swallowed by a raft of Christian apologists. The result of losing contact with the historic Christ is always the same, the "contemporary Christ" created in the image of his human maker. This dogma about history is false, and directly antithetical to the Christian faith. The fact is that we can come to know Jesus Christ historically before we know Him personally. Indeed, we *must*. Otherwise the Christ we know personally is the mirror of our own visage.

Indeed, all the evidence is against form-critical hypothesis. Paul was careful to keep a distinction between his words and those of his Lord (1 Co 7:12). Parables abound in the gospels and are virtually absent from the epistles. Apostlic eyewitnesses governed the church, exercising a control over any myth-making tendencies. The "Son of Man" title is used by Jesus

Himself in the gospels, and is not used of Him in the
epistles. This proves that a clear boundary was respected between the gospels as historical records and
the epistles as church doctrine. The aim of all the
gospels is given by Luke (1:1-4, ASV):

> Forasmuch as many have taken in hand to draw
> up a narrative concerning those matters which have
> been fulfilled among us, even as they delivered them
> unto us, who from the beginning were eyewitnesses
> and ministers of the word, it seemed good to me
> also, having traced the course of all things accurately
> from the first, to write unto thee in order, most
> excellent Theophilus; that thou mightest know the
> certainty concerning the things wherein thou wast
> instructed.

The Jewish procedure of handing down historical
materials was not a haphazard and unorganized accident. The oral tradition was checked by written records, and the written documents were handled with
scrupulous care. This fastidious care is demonstrated
in the transmission of the Hebrew text of the Old
Testament. A comparison of the Isaiah scroll from
the Qumram library with the Isaiah of the Masoretic
text has proved that only the tiniest variations occurred during a full thousand years of copying! It is
entirely possible that Matthew was added to the band
of the disciples because of his training in scribal tech-
niques and kept written notes of the teachings and
activities of Jesus. At any rate there is no basis for
suspecting that the figure of Jesus was a figment of a
communal imagination. Such criticism would reduce
every historical figure to a puff of wind. All that we
ask, is for a person to keep his antisupernatural bias
isolated from his historical integrity if only for the
time it takes to face the person of Jesus Christ fairly.

If we apply the same historical standards to the gospels which we apply to Tacitus and Aristotle, our validation of the Christian message is well on the way.

It is often asked in this connection how much extrabiblical corroboration of the gospels we possess. Often the notion behind this is the belief that the Christian writers are to be held suspect until cleared by nonchristian sources (presumably unbiased). The notion is utterly fallacious, and reverses normal historical procedure. *All* data pertaining to a given question deserves a hearing, and deserves to stand on its own merits. Even if there were not a single piece of extrabiblical attestation, a person would still be confronted with superb historical sources. There is, however, a body of testimonies in Jewish and Gentile writing which touch on the biblical history. The Talmud contains some hostile but historically valuable allusions to the life of Jesus. His followers believed Him virgin-born, He performed miracles, and was executed for heresy. The Jewish historian Josephus fills in many details concerning the rulers mentioned in the New Testament (the Herods, Pilate, Festus, Agrippa), and alluded to the claims of Jesus and the belief in His resurrection. Of the early Gentile writers, Thallus records a solar eclipse during the crucifixion of Christ, but generally the pagan writers had no interest in what they considered to be a vulgar oriental cult. The place to look would be the police records of the Roman Empire if these had survived! Tacitus refers to the great fire of Rome which Nero blamed on the Christians and mentions Christ's execution under Pontius Pilate.

The gospels were written by brave men, many of whom were called upon to die for their historical claims. There was nothing to gain by forgery or deceit. Their works were written in association with eyewitnesses of the events they record, and enjoy a rich textual witness second to none. The gospel message could scarcely possess a sounder historical base by any standard.

10

THE FACT OF CHRIST

THERE EXISTS no document from the ancient world witnessed by so excellent a set of textual and historical testimonies, and offering so superb an array of historical data on which an intelligent decision may be made. An honest man cannot dismiss a source of this kind. Skepticism regarding the historical credentials of Christianity is based upon an irrational bias.

Christianity is Christ. It is only appropriate to begin with Him when investigating the claims of the Christian gospel. He is the center both of our theology and apologetics. In addition, He is almost universally admired and respected for His wisdom, His character, and His beneficial effect upon the world. An intelligent non-Christian owes it to himself to conduct an investigation into the roots of the Christian message, if only to be sure his unbelief is not itself an unfounded prejudice.

Once we open the gospels and encounter Jesus, we are impressed at the enormous difference between the popular concept of Christ and the figure actually portrayed on their pages. Whereas the Christ of modern mythology is a mild-mannered humanist, standing for vague ideals and turning the other cheek to his enemies, the Christ of the New Testament is an intrepid egoist. In every gospel, in almost every chapter, He is found making amazing claims for Himself, which are most shocking if they are not true. He claimed authority over all venerable tradition, He forgave man's sins, He controlled natural forces, He boldly predicted His own resurrection and coming again to judge the world. Eventually the authorities had enough of it and put Him to death for blasphemy. Jesus was not unwilling to die, for He saw death as part of His redeeming mission, but He reiterated time and again that death would not hold Him, and that His resurrection would decisively prove His claims. The ultimate test of His truthfulness lay in a future miracle.

Before developing the nature and importance of Christ's claims, it is necessary to discuss the so-called "quest for the historical Jesus" and the reason for its failure. This quest was the attempt to reconstruct the historical Jesus as He really was. It was often an attempt to delve behind the Christ of myth and dogma, and rediscover the purely human Jesus of Nazareth. The quest ended in hopeless failure, but the reason it did is seldom grasped. It is common to hold that the quest failed because the historical sources for the quest are inappropriate for an inductive scientific investigation, or because the Christ of faith cannot be approached objectively at all. Neither of these reasons is true, however. The gospel accounts are superb historical records on any reckoning and quite capable of yielding positive results. Furthermore, as we have seen already, the essence of the gospel is that the Christ of faith is precisely the Jesus of history and none other. The uniqueness of the Christian message is its open-to-investigation form. The actual reason for failure lies elsewhere. The Jesus of history eluded the historians, not because the sources were "kerygmatic" nor because the incarnation took place in "supra-history," but for the simple reason that a purely human Jesus like they sought never existed! The nineteenth century liberals had decided well in advance of their quest that the only Jesus they were prepared to discover was a naturalistic one. The error in the old quest was not its inductive methodology (that was its virtue), but rather its antisupernatural bias. Of course Jesus eluded their quest since every piece of data we possess presents a divine Messiah. Imagine a quest for the historical Napoleon based on the presumption that every source about his life lied in its fundamental understanding! Such historical pessimism makes the whole science of historiography a ridiculous farce. Seeing correctly the true fallacy of the old quest also gives us the reason why the new quest will fail too. All the new quest has really done is to retain what it ought to have rejected (the naturalistic bias) and rejected what it ought to have retained (the inductive procedure). Its future is not bright. Soon the break with any subject-object distinction will be complete, and the past will entirely vanish. And when the knowledge of the past disappears, men will be condemned to repeat every foolish heresy and error they made before.

But for those uninterested in theological games, and wanting to examine the actual data history bequeaths us, the historical Jesus is not a problem at all. He is less of a problem than Julius Caesar or Alexander the Great. The Christ of the New Testament is readily approachable and rather easier to understand than we would sometimes wish. It is important to begin with Jesus Christ, because it involves no dogmatic preconceptions. Anyone can conduct the simple investigation. However irritating it may be to non-

Christian and existentialist theologian alike, *whosoever will* may come to Jesus, ask Him intelligent questions, and put their trust in Him. Christian evidences merely press the evangelical invitation home to consider *Him*. It was a consideration of the historical facts regarding Jesus Christ that prepared C. S. Lewis to take the gospel seriously. All the evidence of the New Testament points in the same direction — to a Messiah who is both human and divine, and to whom men owe all their allegiance. It matters not whether we read Matthew, Mark, Luke or John, Peter, Paul, James or Jude, the message is the same. The only understanding of Christ which is *not* based upon a speculative reconstruction of the historical materials is one of worship and praise, "My Lord and my God!" The divine Christ is the only Christ of which any document in the New Testament has any knowledge.

"What do you think of the Christ? Whose son is he?" is the question Jesus posed to the people of His day (Mt 22:42). His amazing claims both in words and in action constantly confronted onlookers with the Christological question. When he rode into Jerusalem on a donkey to fulfill the ancient prophecy (Zec 9:9), all the city was stirred to ask, "Who is this?" (Mt 21:10). After Jesus had offered a pardon to the paralytic for his sins, the enemies of Jesus became deeply troubled as they faced the unpalatable alternatives—either He was a dangerous charlatan, or else a divine Messiah (Lk 5:21). The question of Christ's true identity is the most basic in the gospel. Jesus makes a decision inescapable. The whole texture of the gospels is riddled with egocentric teachings. He believed the whole prophetic Scripture was focused on His person (Lk 4:16). The kingdom of God was drawing nigh because He was in the midst of men (Mk

1:15; Lk 17:21). Nothing short of total discipleship was demanded of His followers (Mk 8:34). Otherwise men were not worthy of Him (Mt 10:38). His teachings rang with the great *I AM* statements which are divine claims in structure and content (Ex 3:14; Jn 4:26; 6:35; 8:12; 10:9, 11:25). When one considers that all these claims came from the lips of the humblest of men, his breath is taken away with amazement. Clearly Jesus made direct claims for Himself and His importance. One title He liked to use of Himself was "Son of man." It is drawn from the apocalyptic passage in Daniel (7:13-14) in which the divine figure appears before God and receives a universal kingdom and everlasting dominion. At His trial Jesus forced a decision by deliberately identifying this figure with Himself (Mk 14:62). His coming to earth, however, was structured in two stages: first, as the Servant of the Lord (Is 53) to render sacrifice and satisfaction for the sins of many (Mk 10:45), and second, as the Son of Man (Dan 7) to receive the glory and honor due Him and to reign over men (Mt 16:27, 19:28). At this present time, therefore, men are invited to appropriate the finished work of redemption He performed on behalf of sinners, before the day of grace is exhausted and they must face Him as their Judge (Jn 5:27).

The claims of Jesus were not all direct ones. His assumption of the right to pronounce forgiveness shocked the onlookers (Mk 2:7). Only a miracle could balance the situation (2:9-12). Impressive was the authority with which He taught (Mt 7:28-29) and the claim that His words had eternal validity (Mt 24:35; Jn 12:48). Every one of His miracles had the force of a dramatized claim: healing the sick, casting out demons, stilling the water, multiplying the loaves,

restoring sight, raising the dead. The significance of
these acts was not lost upon those who witnessed and
heard of them. This was an extraordinary divine
Person who had to be reckoned with. The destinies
of all men were suspended on their relationship with
Him.

The person who will consider the claims of Christ
seriously cannot avoid making a decision on the basis
of them. The possible alternatives are not numerous
either. Jesus does not give us much room to move in.
These are shocking alternatives. C. S. Lewis put it this
way:

> A Man who was merely a man and said the sort
> of things Jesus said would not be a great moral
> teacher. He would either be a lunatic—on a level
> with the man who says he is a poached egg—or else
> he would be the Devil of Hell. You must make your
> choice. Either this man was, and is, the Son of God:
> or else a madman or something worse. You can shut
> him up for a fool, you can spit at Him and kill Him
> as a demon; or you can fall at His feet and call
> Him Lord and God. But let us not come with any
> patronising nonsense about His being a great human
> teacher. He has not left that open to us. He did not
> intend to.[1]

Lewis is right. Either a fraud has taken place at
some stage, or else Jesus is the divine Son of God.
The non-Christian cannot avoid claiming a fraud if
he would evade Jesus. But proving it is quite another
matter. The theory that Jesus Himself perpetrated
this fraud, that He was a deceiver, a charlatan, a liar,
a scoundrel, has never appealed to people. It is so
transparently ridiculous. The high level of His ethical
and religious teaching makes any such theory utterly
untenable. It is perhaps possible that He performed

this fraud innocently. Was He deluded about His greatness, a paranoid, an unintentional deceiver, a schizophrenic? Again the skill and depth of His teachings support the case only for His total mental soundness. If only we were as sane as He! No theory that Jesus Christ Himself engineered a deception can stand the test of even a superficial examination. Is it conceivable then that the fraud entered in the years after His death, when His followers began to trump up His importance because they loved Him? This theory suffers from a similar objection. The apostles were simple fishermen, unsophisticated and honest men. Their record of sincerity and teaching does not approve the theory of deception either. They would hardly have been prepared to die for something they themselves had cooked up most deceitfully. Besides, the Messiah they allegedly invented was most unlike any Messiah most people were looking for, and they got the same hostile treatment as their Lord Himself did. Far from wanting to deify Him, His Jewish disciples themselves found that fact hard to accept and did so only under the strongest divine pressures. The people of that day wanted a kingly Messiah, not a suffering Servant; they wanted a human political deliverer, not a divine spiritual Saviour.

The dilemma of Christ's identity will not be easily sidestepped. The most sensible solution is to bow to the force of the evidence for His divinity. Jesus is either guilty of criminal megalomania, or actually the person He claims to be. Once a non-Christian has faced the issue this way, he will not be easily able to shake off his responsibility to decide the issue once and for all.

11

ON THE THIRD DAY

THE CENTRAL MOTIF in the preaching of the earliest disciples was the resurrection of Jesus Christ from death. To them it was the decisive proof that the gospel was true. Here was an event in the stream of world history which boldly demonstrated the existence of God and His intentions for the salvation of men. The fact of the resurrection is an undigestible surd for the naturalist. Yet the birth of the church cannot be explained without this event. It is a focus for both theology and apologetics because it enters into both God's redemptive provision (Ro 4:25) and the ground of certainty (1 Pe 1:3). In addition to laying redemptive groundwork for deliverance, Christ came to demonstrate that the "unknown God" is no longer unknown (Ac 17:23, 31). The resurrection is a fact of history without which history does not make sense. God has acted in the empirical realm, in the flesh and bone of history, in order to save men from both sin and agnosticism. All of the false Messiahs have vanished from history. The only explanation for the existence of the gospel is the bodily resurrection of the Lord.

In considering the fact of the resurrection we come into contact with genuine historical materials. Again we are not interested in *demonstration,* for historical decisions are not capable of such proof. But we are not on that account pessimistic about the value of the evidence. A lawyer, Frank Morrison, set out to write a book disproving the resurrection claim of the Christian church, but the stubbornness of the facts prevented the book from being written. He started out with a bias against the resurrection, but was compelled by honesty to revise his presuppositions. While it is true that historical facticity is not the *only* facet of the resurrection which is important, it is also true that the resurrection is nothing without it. And furthermore, to the non-Christian, factuality is the decisive question, for upon it hangs his decision whether to entrust his life to Christ or not, for time and eternity. The resurrection has tremendous significance for Christian apologetics. It had the same importance for Jesus too. For He literally staked His entire reputation as a teacher of truth upon the prediction that He would rise from the grave (Lk 18:31-33). The integrity of both gospel and Saviour rests upon the validity of this single event.

The validity of the Christian claim turns very much upon the fact of the resurrection on the third day. While recent theological writing contains abundant references to the event, very little in the way of evidence is offered for this crucial datum. Many have sought to hold the Easter faith entirely apart from historical reasoning, and even against it. Knowledge of the resurrection is supposed to come by revelation, not by historical study. In that case it is difficult to understand, first, why the apostles pointed to an event at all, and second, why their testimony matters if the resurrection be "immediately" known. If the *effects* of the resurrection be known, as they are, there is nothing that can stop extrapolating back from the effect to the cause. The motivation behind the attempt to cover over historical evidence is due of course to the upper-story mentality which afflicts theology today.

It is crucial in evangelism and apologetics to have objective considerations to back up the claims for the gospel. The sinner needs to know that the gospel is not the concoction of a human imagination, but is objectively true. The importance of this can be illustrated in an imaginary conversation.

John makes a claim: "I have a five-leaf clover in my room."

Mary challenges it: "I don't believe you. Let's have a look."

John retorts: "Oh it's there all right, but I can't let you see it."

Mary replies: "Why should I believe you when you refuse an investigation?"

Mary's point is well taken. It *is* absurd to claim an objective five-leaf clover on the one hand, and then refuse to contemplate any procedures of verification. No less absurd is the new theology which claims an objective resurrection and then adds that any historical investigation is out of the question. The person who professes the resurrection but denies all objective evidence for it is kidding nobody but himself. No non-Christian will be impressed with such double-talk. His only conclusion will be that such a believer does not hold the resurrection to be a historical fact, but only an existential experience in his own life.

At the forefront of the historical evidence for the supreme miracle of Christianity stands the empty tomb. A scarce three months after the death of Jesus in Jerusalem, His disciples were found proclaiming His bodily resurrection. Very few of the Jewish or

Roman leaders were sympathetic with the new movement which promised to upset the religious balance which had been achieved in Judea with some difficulty. We may safely presume that, had they been able to, they would have successively disproven the Christian claim and nipped the whole movement in the bud. Yet, although the apostles encountered the stiffest opposition to their ministry in Jerusalem, no one was able successfully to falsify their claim that Jesus rose from the grave! The easiest way to have done this would have been to produce the body of Jesus. Neither the Jewish nor the Roman authorities had any motive for keeping it hidden. Apparently it was missing from the tomb in which it had been laid. The Jews invented a story about the disciples stealing the body (Mt 28:11-15) but this obvious fabrication has never carried much weight. Hypocrites do not become martyrs. The disciples might have been deluded, but they were not liars. Besides, there was the practical problem of getting around the guard which Pilate set at the tomb (Mt 27:65). Grave robbers could have been responsible for removing the body except for the absence of any monetary motive for doing so and the same difficulty of breaking the seal and escaping the guards. One of the most decisive proofs for the resurrection is provided unwillingly by the enemies of Jesus who were clearly frustrated in any attempt they made to disprove the claim that Jesus rose.

Various theories of intentional deception on the part of Jesus or the disciples have been proposed in the past. The old swoon theory was that Jesus never actually died on the cross but survived crucifixion, escaped from the tomb, and presented Himself alive to His followers. This theory is harder to believe than the biblical account. It is past belief how Jesus could have survived a crucifixion of six hours and a Roman spear wound, and convinced Pilate and His executioners that He was dead. Then, in a state of terrible physical pain, He endured the coldness of the tomb for three days, removed the large boulder at the door of the grave, eluded the guard posted at the sepulcher, convinced His disciples that He had a glorious resurrection body, and finally disappeared and died in anonymity. A hypothesis of this sort only emphasizes how far a non-Christian will go to escape the inescapable. H. J. Schonfield has a new twist. This deception was in Jesus' mind when He planned to fake death and conjure up a resurrection. He was to receive a pain-killing drug while on the cross to enable Him to survive the ordeal. The whole "Passover plot" fell through, however, when the unexpected happened —a Roman soldier thrust his spear in Jesus' side and the conspiracy was foiled. Aside from the intrinsic improbabilities of Jesus' deliberate deception based on His known character, the theory collapses upon the fact of the empty tomb. How did the conspirators dispose of the body in the end, and convince people the resurrection really happened? The problem remains as big as ever.

Of even greater importance to the disciples in the line of evidences for the resurrection was the series of appearances which the risen Christ made to chosen witnesses (Ac 10:41). Paul gives the earliest list of such appearances (1 Co 15:5-9). The appearance to Peter is put first. Strictly speaking, Christ came first to Mary Magdalene (Jn 20:11-18), but Paul does not wish to include the name of a female in a list which has almost legal force in his mind. The fact that John does record it is impressive because it is a detail

which no first century male would have invented! But
John had the courage to record it, and the story has
important symbolic overtones (cf. Lk 8:2; Mt 27:
55-56). The appearance to Peter and James indi-
vidually and separately goes far to explain their
unique authority in the primitive Jewish church. The
appearance to five hundred brethren at once indicates
the public nature of the evidence. Many of these believers Paul knew to be alive at the time of his writing
(1 Co 15:6). This extensive series of appearances to
many individuals over a period of several weeks is a
phenomenon which calls for an explanation. Jesus left
the clear impression in His disciples that He was
neither the ghost of a dead man nor simply a revived
corpse. He was alive in a new mode of existence, and
He summoned His disciples to proclaim the possibility
of such existence for all who will believe on His name.
These appearances were either actual and substantial,
or else they were hallucinatory. A hallucination is an
apparent perception of an object. It appears frequently
at the end of a period of anxious wishfulness for
something to happen, and to isolated persons, not to
groups. It is striking that all of the factors favorable
to the hallucination hypothesis are absent from the
New Testament. The resurrection caught everyone off
guard. The disciples were surprised and disbelieving
for joy (Mk 16:8; Mt 28:17; Lk 24:36-43; Jn 20:
19). They needed convincing themselves. Jesus did
not come into an atmosphere of wishful thinking.
His appearances occurred at unpredictable times and
in odd places. No psychological gymnastics accompanied them. They just happened. Many had the experience at the same time too, affording correlation
and corroboration. Furthermore, physical aspects to
the appearances, such as His invitation to Thomas

to touch Him, and His eating with the disciples, add to the impressiveness of the appearances. The birth and growth of the early church is utterly inexplicable apart from the appearances of the risen Christ. Only the resurrection itself offers an adequate rational explanation to the facts we see.

There is a fantastic difference between the disciples who appear in the gospel narratives and those who figure in the book of Acts. Timid, unreliable, fearful, unbelieving men emerge from the events immediately following the death of Christ, bursting to tell of His resurrection, whatever the cost to their own personal safety. Peter had returned to his fishing in Galilee (Jn 21:1-3), but later crashed onto the Jerusalem scene to announce the resurrection which he had witnessed (Ac 2:32; 3:15). James had formerly been skeptical (Jn 7:5) but after a resurrection appearance (1 Co 15:7) took the helm of the mother church in Jerusalem (Ac 15:13; Ga 1:19). The entire narrative of the Acts of the Apostles is posited upon this single event. It is woven into its very fabric. The disciples were intellectually convinced that the gospel was true, because God had raised Jesus from the dead. The conversion of Paul from his bitter hostility to the Christian movement in the beginning to his energetic defense of the gospel all around the Mediterranean world is further testimony to the resurrection. It was the only appearance Christ made to an avowed enemy of His. "Nothing but a sudden, unexpected, objective, irresistible revelation of the Resurrected One Himself in the majesty of his divine power could convince and convert a man like Saul. It was such an appearance which was given him," wrote D. A. Hayes. Paul's entire ministry thereafter is massive testimony to the reality of Christ's resurrection.

There are very few events of ancient history better attested with sound evidence than the resurrection of Jesus Christ. It is as secure in its place in the annals of history as almost any other event. The resurrection is the only hypothesis which will make peace with all the facts. It constitutes excellent motivation for trusting Christ. Its evidence is sufficiently impressive to demand an answer from every non-Christian. The documentary evidence is superb. Few facts enjoy such corroboration. The resurrection stands within the realm of historical factuality.

12

SOLA SCRIPTURA

THE CHRISTIAN MESSAGE is historical to the core. All of its doctrines arise from God's self-disclosure in history. Its doctrine of authority, therefore, is given in the disclosure situations of redemptive history; that is, the nature of Scripture is determined from the teachings of divinely authenticated messengers, Jesus Christ and His apostles. The entire edifice of theology is built upon this epistemological foundation. Without the propositional revelation in Scripture, theology is an impossible endeavor; and yet, acceptance of biblical authority is not an unfounded assumption. The work of the theologian does not hang from a skyhook. The resurrection of Jesus Christ establishes His truthfulness in all things. The evangelical doctrine of authority is grounded in the God-given teachings (Jn 7:16) of the risen Lord Himself. His view of Scripture must be the view of His disciples. The Bible is not infallible because *it* says so—but because *He* says so. There is no more reliable witness to the nature of Scripture than the one who died and rose to be our Saviour. According to Jesus, divine revelation is mediated in a written record with the authority of God speaking. What the Scripture says, God says (Mt 5:18; 19:4; Jn 10:34; Ac 4:25; 28:25;

Heb 10:15). Whether or not we receive the testimony to Scripture as an infallible record of God's revelation is a commentary on the consistency of our Christian discipleship. It is not difficult to understand a biblical critic doubting the veracity of the Scripture who cares nothing for its divine Saviour, but it is strange to find a believer professing his Lord and then disregarding Christ's doctrine of inspiration. The authority of Scripture rests upon the datum of the incarnation. As soon as a person comes to faith in the divine Son of God, the question of authority is settled.

Until relatively recent times, Christians have seen the logic of this pattern of authority. The Lord rules His church by the Word and Spirit. Scripture was the ground for believing revealed truths. Now all of that has changed. A destructive principle has been admitted, the *dichotomy* of biblical errancy. If something is taught in Scripture, it may *or* may not be true. In other words, Scripture is not the ground for believing anything. If the Bible errs in minor matters, perhaps it errs also in major ones; if in incidental things, perhaps in substantial things as well. In the past, the battle lines were fairly closely drawn between the skeptics on the one hand who charged errors and defects in Scripture, and believers on the other hand who stoutly resisted such allegations. Now the average biblical critic who is a member of a Christian church is glad to admit the skeptic's charges and puts up little resistance to his assaults. The reason for this about face is the disengagement from history noted in chapter 2. The new theologian is so afraid of uncertainty in historical research that he immunizes his gospel from all contact with the "facts." His *kerygma* is capable only of subjective validation and neither errors in biblical history nor fallacies in biblical doctrine bother him anymore. But they *ought* to bother him! The credibility of the Christian message is bound up with the reliability of its historical proclamation. The very integrity of Jesus Christ rests on the truths of His doctrine of authority. There is no real alternative to the dilemma, either a divine Saviour and an infallible Bible, or a fallible Bible and no divine Saviour. From the documents alone it is possible to learn that they are reliable to a substantial degree (see chap. 9), but from Jesus Christ we learn their divinely inspired nature. Their general reliability is a matter of public fact; their infallibility is a doctrine revealed through Jesus Christ.

For many today, however, the question of what Jesus Christ taught about Scripture cannot be seriously faced because the evidence against biblical infallibility is so overwhelming that it is hardly relevant. Negative biblical criticism has conducted a wide campaign of brainwashing to this effect. Irresponsible spokesmen contend that no intelligent person could hold to a concept of verbal inspiration. It would require intellectual suicide to believe in biblical inerrancy. It is a silly idolatry and an absurd rationality, they say. All this talk is very intimidating to the young Christian until he stumbles upon one piece of unadmitted information. The "errors" of the Bible are a very slippery lot. Just when you have your hands on one, it evades you and disappears. At bottom these "errors" are really only *difficulties masquerading as errors*. In 1800 the French Institute in Paris issued a list of eighty-two errors in the Bible which they believed would destroy Christianity. Today none of these "errors" remain! With further reflection and new discoveries, these "errors" were cleared away. Surely it will be so with all such difficulties. We have our

Saviour's word for that. Criticism has unquestionably made some advances in the understanding of Scripture. But in its speculative theories in the field of higher criticism, there have been many reversals. The real question is: When does a difficulty become an error? The critics claimed a host of "errors" in 1850 which were recanted by 1950. The existence of the Hittites who were an "error" in 1900 are not even a problem today, due to archeological finds. It is imperative to distinguish between a difficulty not-yet-solved and an "error." Errors are inconsistent with an infallible Bible, but difficulties are *not*. A little humility on the part of the critic, and a little more corroboration on the part of the archeologist and linguist may change the picture entirely. The evangelical Christian is well aware that unsolved difficulties exist in the biblical text, but he is unwilling for that reason alone to make a rash verdict about biblical infallibility. His doctrine of Scripture, like all his beliefs, derives not from his independent research, but from the doctrine of Scripture his Lord has advanced. Belief in biblical infallibility ought not to be jettisoned because difficulties are known to exist in the text. On the authority of Jesus Christ we have the assurance that these "errors" are far more apparent than real.

Confidence in the happy outcome of biblical research is not blind trust. The number of significant reversals in biblical criticism in the past one hundred years has been extensive. A century ago the book of Genesis was considered a hopeless collection of unsubstantiated myths. Moses, it was thought, would have been unable to write. The Hittites had never existed. The literature was put together with scissors and paste at the hands of fairly unintelligent ancient bookmakers. Then the avalanche of discovery in the Near East came to bury these preposterous theories. Egyptian and Hittite parallels turned up in abundance. Personal names and customs were found echoed in the Amarna letters, the Nuzi tablets, and the Ugaritic texts. The fanciful criteria for discerning literary strands in the documents of the Pentateuch have been subjected to severe criticism, and abandoned by many. Writing in the Near East was already a well-established art in the second millennium B.C. If critics continue to point to Genesis with allegations of "error" they will do so despite the evidence, not because of it.

The book of Deuteronomy provides another striking example. For some years a sixth century date for the book of Deuteronomy has been regarded as an assured result of criticism. It was alleged to be the book read aloud to King Josiah in connection with his reform of religion. On such a view, the book, which depicts the later life and teachings of Moses, is fraudulent. However, the recent discovery of historical data has emphasized the antiquity and authenticity of Deuteronomy. Its entire historical and theological stance is manifestly premonarchy. But the discovery of the Hittite covenant codes at Hattusa and other vassal treaties from Assyrian and Aramaic sources has contributed factual evidence for a radical reversal. For the similarity of these treaties to the literary structure of Deuteronomy is striking: preamble, historical prologue, stipulations, sanctions, dynastic disposition. The comparison indeed compels us to recognize that the origin of Deuteronomy *as a unit* lies in the second millennium, not in the first. The facts are opposed to the modern critical theory, and demand a reconsideration.

The book of Daniel too has suffered much in the critics' den. It has been taken for a thinly disguised forgery purporting to describe the events of the fifth century B.C. while actually reflecting on the events of the second. Historical blunders and linguistic anachronisms were referred to as proof of pseude-pigraphy. The facts, however, point in a different direction. The discovery of the Elephantine papyri makes it difficult to lay much stress on the Aramaic of Daniel, and our knowledge of the early contacts between the Greek and Palestinian civilizations naturally explains the presence of Greek loanwords in the text of Daniel. Better knowledge of the neo-Babylonian and Persian periods has largely cleared up the historical problems. The fresh evidence backing a strong view of biblical authenticity ought to encourage the' believer under heavy pressure from critical propaganda. Other Old Testament examples of reversals could easily be cited. Suffice it to say criticism is in great flux, and "errors" in the Bible cannot be easily charged. Biblical critics have often been hasty in their skepticism and uncontrolled in their speculations. If they are not prepared to revise their theories in the light of the new evidence, then it is they, and not the so-called "conservatives," who have their heads in the sand.

There are several notable examples of critical reversals in the New Testament too. One example is the book of Acts. In the last century the work was considered by many to be a second century fabrication of the history of the first, a romance designed to cover up the Petro-Pauline rift in the primitive church. The theory was not constructed on factual evidence but on a Hegelian mythology of history. Sir William Ramsay, who at first was taken in by the hypothesis, decided to test it out on the field in the Near East. The *facts* utterly changed his presuppositions. His research into the archeological data convinced him of Luke's reliability, and converted him to the authenticity of Acts.

The gospel of John experienced a similar fortune at the hands of the critics. At first the work was taken to be a pious fiction, written by a well-meaning admirer of Jesus, but having no value as a historical source. The situation has entirely reversed itself today. It has been recognized that John is the most Jewish gospel of the four and contains numerous details which suggest its author was an eyewitness. His accurate knowledge of Palestinian custom, history, and geography almost demand that the writer was himself a native of Palestine and a participant in the events he records.

These few examples show how precarious criticism of biblical infallibility is. For until the interpreter is omniscient and all the evidence comes in, it is impossible to press the theory of "inductive errancy." We ought neither to undererstimate our task (for there remains much homework yet to be done), nor to overestimate its size (for it is nowhere nearly as large as the propaganda suggests). Difficulties in Scripture do not overthrow the infallibility principle. They are but mountains yet to be scaled and lands yet to be conquered.

13

THE LIVING GOD

THE WHOLE GOSPEL MESSAGE is grounded on one basic postulate: the existence of the sovereign triune God, who is both infinite and personal. Christian theology without this God is as inconceivable to contemplate as geology without rocks or anthropology without man. Until recently the line was rather sharply drawn between atheism and theism at the point of God's existence. This is now no longer the case. Paul's principle of all things to all men has been extended to include the secular gospel. We are to address man in his secularity, and not require of him metaphysical beliefs foreign to his milieu. An ecumenical bridge has been thrown across the chasm of atheism and theism. Dialogue is encouraged between Christians and Marxists, Catholics and Buddhists, theists and humanists. Man and his concerns are so at the center of all contemporary thinking that God and His nature can be set aside as an indeterminate quantity. The rise to prominence of the theothanatologists (the "death-of-god" theologians) has only contributed to the ambiguity of His existence in the minds of many. The theoretical efforts of the theological morticians, together with the secular way of life today, combine to make the question a practical irrelevance.

Biblical religion approaches the question of God's existence from the angle of history. Its entire thrust arises from the claim that the living God has *shown Himself* in historical events which cannot otherwise be explained than by acknowledging His existence. We have already noted how the new theology, whether it be existentialist or rationalistic, finds this aspect repugnant. Not enough certainty resides in history to support their conception of religion. The gospel notwithstanding does make her validity rest upon actual historical occurrences. The apostles did *not* witness to what God had done in the resurrection simply in order to indicate what God was doing in their lives. They appealed to the record of history because they believed it would yield evidence to the impartial observer of the truth of the gospel. The apostles had no wish to escape criticism on this score. They were convinced Jesus' rising was a plain fact, and did not fear close examination. For the Old and New Testaments, history is the medium in which revelation has unmistakably occurred. Faith and knowledge go hand in hand. Faith lays hold on the fact of Christ risen, and faces the future in the light of this. It is the structure of the biblical religion which determines its approach to the question of God's existence.

However, Scripture does not stop there. It does not suggest that those who have not been exposed to the light of historical revelation exist in some kind of theological limbo. On the contrary it boldly asserts that all men everywhere are always confronted with the fact of God's existence (Ps 19:1; Ro 1:18-25). It has been observed that nowhere does Scripture attempt a deductive argument for the existence of God like those of Thomas Aquinas, for example. This fact ought not to be taken to imply, however, that such an effort is unjustifiable and necessarily useless. The distinctiveness of the biblical approach is its *immediacy*. The theistic proofs for God's existence constitute a laborious, painstaking and patient justification of theism. They attempt to set forth in rational argument what the soul grasps intuitively. But for the Bible the deepest proof of God's existence is just life itself. The knowledge of God and man's knowledge of himself are closely intertwined. If only God could be written off neatly and cleanly, how simple things would be. But the hound of heaven pads after us all. He does not let us go. There is no escaping Him. At the moment when least expected He closes in. The explanation for this is man's creation in the image of God (Gen 1:26). His identity is known theologically, in relation to the God who is. Man in his true significance cannot survive permanently in isolation from his Maker. Without God, man is the chance product of unthinking fate and of little worth. The current loss of identity and the emergence of the faceless man in today's culture are testimony to the effects of losing our God. The knowledge of God is given in the same movement in which we know ourselves.

Paul taught too that the natural order witnesses to the existence of an infinite personal God (Ro 1:19-20). The world is stamped with His trademark. It is an artifact constructed by an invisible Craftsman. It is impossible, the apostle states, to avoid the conclusion that an almighty power exists apart from the visible order. Man's condition of low visibility is not due to the absence of evidence for God's existence, but to his own blindness, which is related to the sin problem. It is imperative to notice that Scripture *never* connects unbelief to the IQ or the lack of sound evidence; for there are reasons adequate for all. Unbelief is rather

due to man's willful autonomy and refusal to bow
before the living God. He is without excuse. The data
present in the natural order which testifies to God's
reality get through to every man, but his reaction to
them is conditioned by his state of soul. Because he
is a covenant-breaker and enemy of God (Ro 8:7-8;
2 Co 4:4), his receiving gear dulls, deflects and
perverts the testimony that comes. Though he is more
an atheist in lip than life, he continues to resist the
still small voice of God. He lives as if it were true,
while denying it is so. It is difficult to live with the
implications of the belief that in the beginning matter
created the heavens and the earth, whether scientifically, philosophically or morally. And he does not
live with them, but daily cheats against his presuppositions. The world is not a mechanistic cage and
man knows it. God speaks from within man's nature
as created in the image of God and summons him
back to the Father's house.

In Romans 2 Paul adds another pointer to God's
existence within the consciousness of man: "Where-
fore thou art without excuse, O man, whosoever thou
art that judgest: for wherein thou judgest another,
thou condemnest thyself; for thou that judgest dost
practise the same things" (v 1, ASV). Paul does not
claim here that all men have the same moral codes.
They do not. Where man is his own lawgiver and
where a moral warp exists in his soul, we could not
expect the law of God to emerge unsullied in his
systems of ethics. Paul merely claims that all men
have moral *motions*. They set up standards of behavior, condemm others for not keeping to them, and
turn around to violate them themselves. Man is condemned within the circle of his own consciousness. No
man at the judgement can say, "I did not know." The

divine tribunal sits in every human heart. The prominence of sacrifice in the religions of the world is proof
of a guilty conscience and the desperate attempt to
atone for sin. Men know their position before a holy
God.

For the Scripture then, the existence of God is both
a historical truth (God acted into history), and an
existential truth (God reveals Himself to every soul).
His existence is both objectively and subjectively evident. It is necessary *logically* because our assumption
of order, design and rationality rests upon it. It is
necessary *morally* because there is no explanation for
the shape of morality apart from it. It is necessary
emotionally because the human experience requires
an immediate and ultimate environment. It is necessary *personally* because the exhaustion of all material
possibilities still cannot give satisfaction to the heart.
The deepest proof for God's existence apart from
history is just life itself. God has created man in His
image, and man cannot elude the implications of this
fact. Everywhere their identity pursues them. Ultimately there is no escape. "Whither shall I go from
thy spirit? or whither shall I flee from thy presence?
If I ascend up into heaven, thou art there: if I make
my bed in hell, behold, thou art there." (Ps 139:7-8).

14

THE GRAND MYTH .

EVERY GENERATION has its myths, and it is always easier to detect the myths of other cultures than our own. A myth is a story which offers an imaginary explanation for the origin and shape of life. So pervasively does it envelop the culture, and so exactly does it coincide with the contemporary spirit, that its inner absurdities go almost unnoticed. Anyone who would dare to dispute it is considered foolish. All educated people in the twelfth century knew the earth was flat. No other possibility was even considered. Evolution is the cultural myth of the twentieth century. It offers to provide a total explanation of all reality without requiring man to answer to the God of creation. It is religious to the core. Undoubtedly, different lines of evidence are adduced which attempt to establish its factual basis, but these do not begin to explain the tenacity of the myth. Its pertinence to Christian apologetics is far deeper than is commonly admitted. Evolution in our day represents the attempt to furnish a total world view into which all reality will neatly fit. It places the whole phenomenal world, the realm of sense data, under the umbrella of naturalism, and leaves religion with the noumenal realm, the upper story, about which we can know nothing but believe much. Since science is a sacred cow, we must tread softly. But it is imperative to insist that the attempt to ground reality in a naturalistic theory of origins *cannot* be done. It is impossible to assume in the light of current knowledge that order sprang out of bare chaos and life emerged spontaneously. Evolutionary dogmatism springs from religious a prioris and not from proven facts. On the contrary, it imputes a bigger miracle to dead matter than the one creation requires. The root question to be answered is this: Does creativity rest with God or nature? Has God ordained the decree in which all things work together (Eph 1:11; Ro 8:28) or has random chance through physical causation effected this? The choice is between Darwin's theory and the biblical God.

Men of almost every generation have believed themselves to be at the apex of knowledge. This makes the myths especially difficult to expose. Scientifically the concept of evolution has almost outworn its usefulness. So many inner contradictions have been pointed out that the hypothesis has ceased to be helpful. Yet the brainwashing goes on. High school textbooks, educational TV science programs, and the popular press continue to play on men's gullibility. Evolution (as if the term conveys a precise entity) is presented "as it happened." Charts and illustrations of life's progress over millions of years are shown. It would almost lead one to believe the magazine had live coverage! All of this despite the admitted fact that no scientist has come anywhere near demonstrating an unbroken line of evolution with any certainty. It is totally irresponsible to give the impression to students that evolution (whatever that means) is a demonstrated fact, or even a secure hypothesis. One can only conclude that the ruling intelligentsia have some motive for pushing this myth and converting our people to it. The motive is not difficult to discern. For the myth allows secular man to retain his autonomy without losing his freedom, or so they hope. Quite obviously the solution is not without nonscientific problems too. There is a severe tension between nature and freedom, as Hermann Dooyeweerd has pointed out. For a mechanical nature which runs on the lines of physical causation cannot easily become the mother of free and significant human beings. The two motifs clash with one another in a new form of the age-old paradox between freedom and determinism. But modern man needs his myth badly. Nature is his mother and her laws his principles, because he will not have God to reign over him. Yet freedom is his hope because otherwise he is a machine too. And so he is caught between two total and contradictory claims. Yet he prefers this tension to acknowledging the rights of the King. Indeed he sets up his own nonchristian upper and lower story. In the lower story he keeps his nature with its omnipotent decree, and in the upper story he guards his pretended autonomy and religion. And despite the sheer irrationality of this structure that random selection should have produced freedom, order and purpose, and that the entire event is one vast insurrection against the second law of thermodynamics, he hangs onto his precious myth. For freedom even in these chains is better, he thinks, than bondage to God.

Fundamentally evolution is an antiscientific myth. It is more a philosophy than a hypothesis. It makes man king at the top of the evolutionary pile, and promises him a nice man-made paradise at the end of the journey, an exquisite counterfeit of the biblical faith. But the myth is antiscientific. Dr. G. L. Jepsen, professor of vertebrate paleontology at Princeton University, remarked: "What we need are more competent fossils. We have plenty of competent anthropologists, but not nearly enough specimens." Much evolutionary thinking is entirely speculative and nonscientific. The current popularity of Teilhard de Chardin, with the backing of the high priest of the church scientific, Julian Huxley, is a case in point. His work is not successful because his facts are new or soundly based, but because the world is ready for the myth he projects. In fact, his entire theory of hominid history suffers from a whole series of missing links, and the proof for the grand hypothesis is almost totally lacking. Dr. William L. Strauss, Jr., professor of physical anthropology at Johns Hopkins University, commented, "The direct, or fossil, evidence for primate and hence for human evolution is relatively scanty and largely incomplete, too frequently consisting of mere fragments or even only teeth." Evolution succeeds not because it is a sound theory, but because it bolsters the humanistic faith which modern man has foolishly adopted in place of the Christian gospel. It persists despite nature, not because of her. But we face a church scientific whose propaganda has made even the truth sound strange. Evolution in its scientific aspects is a string on which data are suspended. With a fertile imagination and a little stretching, a case for it can be made out. But the harmony of the data with this theory exists largely in the mind of modern secular man who is blind to any other possibility. This is not a skirmish in the warfare between science and religion. Evolutionary science is as religious as religion is. If we jump on this bandwagon, we will do so not because the facts compel us but because we want to. The real warfare between valid empirical science which

stays within the field of legitimate inferences from data
and which allows for the possibility of the biblical
world view, and this pseudo science has scarcely be-
gun. The assumption of the spontaneous origin of
life is just about as reasonable as an explosion in a
printing plant resulting in the twenty-four volumes of
the *Encyclopaedia Britannica.* The theory rests on
inadequate factual grounds and there is reason for
real doubt that it is a valid theory at all.

Sigmund Freud ran into one of the thorniest problems in evolution—genetics. As as atheist and naturalist, Freud was compelled to adopt the myht in
some form. But he could not bring himself around to
accepting the myth in its Darwinian version because
that involved natural selection. He felt that for natural
selection to account for such a godlike creature as
man was too big a miracle. So he admired Lamarck's
theory of acquired characteristics until the end of his
life, a fact which has embarrassed his biographers
ever since. Lamarck offered him a possible mechanism
for upward development which blind chance could not
provide. However, Lamarck's hypothesis has been
decisively disproven. Proficiency gained by the parent
is not passed on to the child. Heredity depends upon
gene chemistry, not intelligence. The fact of the matter
is that genetics is opposed to *both* Darwin and
Lamarck. For although microevolution can be observed within certain limits, this freedom is strictly
controlled, and the genetic foundation between Darwin's theory of chance variations reproducing themselves is very weak if not nonexistent. The science of
genetics has yet to supply a convincing explanation for
the emergence of animal and plant groups. The example of Freud merely illustrates the dilemmas in and
the confused state of current evolutionary thought.

Every theory so far requires a miracle somewhere along the way greater than creation itself.

The myth is not without its tragic overtones, for it epitomizes the trapped position of man. In his self-understanding man is but the accidental product of blind chance. He is caught in an impersonal causal nexus. Chance and fate are back of everything. There is no qualitative difference between man and a stone. Man is the most miserable creature in the universe, his identity lost, and his personality smothered by the weight of a "paneverythingism," in which the fittest, not the noblest, are the gods. Little wonder that he is seeking a return to chaos for salvation. For chaos, he believes, is the fountainhead of all reality, the source of all creativity and reality. Like the Saturnalia cult in ancient Rome, he desires a return to formlessness and lawlessness. He hopes that by negating law and order by violent revolution in every field he will find a paradise tomorrow. He derives his hope from his myth. But the hope cannot materialize because reality is not this way. He is trapped in the horror of decreation, trusting in a myth which is scientifically dubious and philosophically nihilistic.

In America science is messianic. Scientists are priests and prophets of the current mythology. Often they speak as oracles of the new divinity. The problem this raises for Christians has little relation to actually demonstrated facts, but springs from a habit of thinking. The issue at bottom is the philosophy of science which today would play the role of infallible interpreter of all reality. Science is far from neutral. Evolution is her controlling concept, the framework which she assumes and within which she works. "What my net won't catch isn't fish." If this fact will not fit my theory, so much the worse for the fact! It represents

a categorical denial of the biblical revelation. The
theistic assertion of the gospel is excluded from the
start. The only theory that will receive serious thought
is one which can make peace with a naturalistic interpretation of the data. The Christian must be prepared
to attack the basic presuppositions of current pseudo
science, and insist that creativity rests with God, not
nature. The Christian explanation of the origin of
reality in the fiat creation of God deserves careful
consideration. It frees the scientist from the need to
provide an all-embracing theory of origins which his
data simply will not sustain, and provides him with a
stable world view in which his researches have solid
foundations. But the Christian interpretation of reality
is not an arbitrary, solipsistic hypothesis, like the in-
terpretations of man. For, if Jesus Christ really rose
from the grave, his interpretation of reality is certainly
the correct one. The risen Christ is the focal point for
all valid historical and scientific interpretation. "Where
wast thou when I laid the foundations of the earth?"
(Job 38:4; cf. Col 1:16).

15

A CONSISTENT APPROACH

A CERTAIN WOMAN named Lydia, . . . whose heart the Lord opened to give heed unto the things which were spoken by Paul" (Ac 16:14, ASV). Successful evangelism requires an inner and an outer event, the cooperation of a divine and a human witness. An evangelist must convey saving truth to the soul, and the Spirit must create the capacity to receive it. In saving men Jesus Christ employs two agents: the Holy Spirit in regeneration and conviction, and men in the presentation of the gospel. The outer testimony is used by the Spirit to create saving faith. He provides the inward confirmation that the message, understood intellectually, is true. Christian apologetics is concerned with the outer event, the role of the human witness. It goes almost without saying that apart from the work of the Spirit the gospel itself could only be truth on ice, cold and fruitless. The reason for this is traced back to the resistance of the natural man to the truth (Ac 7:51; 1 Co 2:14). The gospel itself, however, is solidly rooted in history and fact. It is our task to present a cogent testimony to its truthfulness.

Apologetic methodology ought to reflect faithfully and consistently a biblical theology. Man is finite and sinful. His reason is not ultimate in the universe. His mind is also fallen and twisted (Eph 4:18). He needs

119

both revelation for his finiteness and regeneration for
his sinfulness. It will be forever impossible for man
to explain the meaning of reality starting from himself alone. The Bible teaches that reality will not yield
her secrets except on the basis of the Christian God
and His revelation. Any other clue to the meaning of
the universe is bound to prove frustrating and disap-
pointing. Man's reason comes to real fruition when it
acknowledges the self-revealing God and is regener-
ated. There can therefore be no naive presenting of
the evidences for Christianity. A witness must be given
and the data adduced, but the Spirit must be present
to act upon the truth if it is to be effective. The problem in apologetics is not the validity of the truth but
its reception. The mind is like a sieve through which
all the facts pass. They are sorted out in categories according to the shape of thought in the mind. The non-
christian interprets everything in accord with his naturalistic set of premises. Lumps of truth may get stuck
in the sieve, but nothing will finally convert a person
until the sieve itself is shattered.

This shattering in the last analysis is the work of
the Spirit. The conviction of guilt, the radical unmasking of the sinner, is his task. "He will reprove
the world of sin" (Jn 16:8). It is humanly impossible
to do this. Yet there is a human role in the process
of "elenctics." It is the role of prophetic preaching,
the exposing of the gospel. For underneath all the
argumentation and self-denial lies the basic sin of
fleeing the living God. The negative side to apologetics,
the radical unmasking, is part of the offense in evangelism. For it challenges the pretended autonomy of
man-centered thinking. Man is not big enough to be
his own *arche* (starting point). The fear of the Lord
is the only *arche* of wisdom (Pr 1:7). The non-Chris-

tian needs to be challenged to carry his starting point
through in all his life and thinking if he can, and see
where it leads him. It will lead him invariably to the
breaking point. Meaning cannot be achieved apart from
the gospel. In Christ "are hid all the treasures of
wisdom and knowledge" (Col 2:3). The whole structure derived from and depends on Him. From the
starting point of man's ultimacy and independence no
progress can be made. Man cannot comprehend reality
or himself from this point of departure. The finite
mind cannot avoid a confession of bankruptcy. Any
presentation of Christian evidences must be accompanied by a radical unmasking. There is no place in
the universe for man to stand unless the Christian
God exists.

> According to an old tale, certain clever philoso-
> phers approached an emperor, offering to weave for
> him a rare and costly garment which would have
> the marvelous capacity of making known to him
> the fools and knaves in his realm. Because of the
> magic quality of the threads, the garment would be
> invisible to all but the wise and the pure in heart.
> Delighted, the emperor commissioned the weaving
> of the royal robes at great cost, only to find to his
> dismay, that he obviously was a fool and knave for
> he saw nothing on the looms. On the day set for the
> grand parade, the knavish philosophers collected
> their royal fee, dressed the emperor in his pot-bellied
> nakedness, and skipped out of town as the parade
> began. The whole populace joined the couriers in
> praising the king's garments, none daring to admit
> that they saw nothing but the emperor's nudity, lest
> they be branded as self-admitting fools and knaves.
> The entire parade of folly collapsed, as the shame
> of king and people was exposed by a child's honest
> remark, "The emperor has no clothes!"

The story has often been retold, with no small homilies on the feelings of king and people. But, significantly, the boy has been neglected, as truth usually is. Consider the future of that boy: with one small truth, he exposed a national and personal lie. With a grain of truth, he turned a people's glory into shame. It is no wonder nothing is said of him. The knavish philosophers got off scott free, and rich as well. Emperor and people went on with their everyday activities, eating, drinking, marrying and giving in marriage. But the small boy was to old age an outcast: he had told the truth and and shamed his race. Not only the king's nakedness, but that of his people, even of his father and mother, had been exposed to the public gaze by his truth. None were consciously naked until this truth destroyed their lie, ripping away their fig-leaf of common hypocrisy.[1]

Everybody's pride was hurt. He could have broken the truth gradually and in pieces. He showed utter lack of tact. But that situation, and our own, calls for forthrightness, not diplomacy. According to the Bible the nonchristian positions are deceptive and self-defeating. It is high time for a prophetic voice to be raised in the name of Christ against the vanity of man-centered thinking and the need for intellectual repentance. Apologetics has been sleeping long enough, afraid of its own shadow and of a direct confrontation. "I have set before you life and death . . . choose life" (Deu 30:19).

All men employ the rational function. They are capable of receiving and evaluating data. Because of the noetic effects of sin, however, the non-Christian is unwilling to allow the truth of the gospel to have its persuasive effect in his life. The miracle of regeneration coincident with the presentation of the gospel is required in order to convert him to Christ. The faith which the Spirit creates in the heart is an intelligent faith, and we must fulfill our role of bringing to the attention of people the grounds of faith. For all men live in God's world and cannot succeed in their attempt to root all things back into chance. At some point they cheat, and live as if the gospel were true. Our strategy must be to stalk our prey, to plot his intellectual and moral position, and to close in with that which may heal his wounds and release him from captivity. The radical unmasking must take place.

There is a cafeteria of clues to the meaning of the universe. Men do adopt a set of presuppositions in order to sort out the avalanche of facts which confront them in reality. Often these premises are not examined. However, the history of ideas shows us clearly that great thinkers have frequently been known to exchange one set of presuppositions for another. In time it can become apparent that an earlier set of axioms no longer does the job and requires significant alteration. People are converted from one ideology to another daily. The non-Christian is operating on a naturalistic set of premises. Without the work of the Spirit he is unlikely to change them, not, however, because the Christian presuppositions are not truer and better in every way, but because he has no *will* to. Christian apologetics is called upon to challenge the validity of the nonchristian starting point, and to offer a far better one. God has broken into history in the person of Jesus Christ. The data are there for all to examine. We must challenge the non-Christian to suspend his prejudice against Christianity for the time it takes to examine fairly the evidence for the Christian faith, to take up a proven method for ascertaining truth, the empirical method, and apply it to the biblical records. No one is imprisoned within an iron cage of presuppositions. By the truth of the gospel and through the power of the Spirit he can be freed.

John Warwick Montgomery tells a revealing story in this connection:

> Once upon a time there was a man who thought he was dead. His concerned wife and friends sent him to the friendly neighbourhood psychiatrist. The psychiatrist determined to cure him by convincing him of one fact that contradicted his belief that he was dead. The psychiatrist decided to use the simple truth that dead men do not bleed. He put his patient to work reading medical texts, observing autopsies, etc. After weeks of effort, the patient finally said, "All right, all right! You've convinced me. Dead men do not bleed." Whereupon the psychiatrist stuck him in the arm with a needle, and the blood flowed. The man looked down with a contorted, ashen face and cried: "Good Lord! Dead men bleed after all!"[2]

Montgomery goes on to comment astutely:

> This parable illustrates that if you hold unsound presuppositions with sufficient tenacity, facts will make no difference at all, and you will be able to create a world of your own, totally unrelated to reality and totally incapable of being touched by reality. Such a condition (which the philosophers call solipsistic, psychiatrists call autistically psychotic, and lawyers call insane) is tantamount to death because connection with the living world is severed. The man in the parable not only thought he was dead, but in a very real sense, he *was* dead because facts no longer meant anything to him.[3]

Undoubtedly such men exist for whom Christian evidences hold no interest or cogency. Until their own ship of state breaks up on the rocks of irrational absurdity, they will not open their ears to the good

news. But the majority of men are not so. They still
seek a haven of rest, not in the leap of ungrounded
faith, but in commitment to the historical verities of
the gospel.

CONCLUSION:

THE EVANGELICAL IMPERATIVE

THE DECISION of an intelligent man is based upon rational considerations. Choosing one's world view is not a game of Russian roulette. Our generation is sick of autobiographical theology in which nothing comes to the surface except personal prejudices. The root factor in the Christian message is its appeal to history. The destruction of historical objectivity and the elimination of the essential subject-object distinction have proved fatal to Christian apologetics. The counter-attack must be on a wide front. Faith which floats around in a sea of untestable assertions is empty and deceptive. The purpose of apologetics is to remove prejudice against the gospel and to lay a solid basis for faith in it. People are constantly affected in their actions and choices by arguments, intelligent or otherwise. The notion that nobody is ever converted to Christ by argument is a foolish platitude. It would be more accurate to say that the reason so few people are being converted to Him now is that so many Christians believe the fallacy. It is high time for us to restock the arsenal of Christian evidences and confront our contemporaries with a solid message. Christians who are addicted to the existential divorce from reality are lazy witnesses. In a world which is increasingly alienated from the body of divine revelation, a "faith in faith" solution will not meet the need, and sinners will not hear the gospel. The hour has struck for a renaissance in Christian letters, and the training of a body of articulate apologists. We need a group of well-trained scholars capable of following the myths of our day to their source, and exposing them there. Their ministry would include traveling from city to city, and university to university, defending the whole faith and presenting the evidence for its validity. Out of their midst would come a library of new literature in every area of theological concern, which would spark a revival in life and truth throughout the length and breadth of the Christian church. Ours is a day of specialization. Men are preoccupied with the minutiae in science and history. We sadly lack men who understand the broad sweep of the contemporary intellectual climate, and who can relate the gospel intelligently to it. To do this, the boundary lines between various disciplines must be crossed bravely, and the connections drawn which illuminate the entire field of human thought. Until this is done, our apologetics will be piecemeal and unconvincing.

The usefulness of Christian apologetics goes far beyond evangelism and personal soul-winning. It also fills the believer's heart with joy as he contemplates the factuality and truth of his faith. What an encouragement to know with mind and emotions that our salvation is grounded in objective reality! Christianity is a historical religion. Evidences are therefore important to it. They do not convert the soul; they do distinguish faith from mere gullibility. This places a heavy weight of responsibility upon the shoulders of educated Christians. For they have a ministry to the whole church of demonstrating that the ground of its

faith is sound. This aspect of the gift of teaching has
been sadly lacking in the body of Christ for some
time now. The moment has come to revive this gift
within our midst and place much strenuous effort behind the defense of the faith. For besides being a
potent weapon in our evangelistic thrust, it is the
life preserver that can rescue our Christian young
people drowning in the sea of uncertainty. The beauty
of the gospel is its facticity. But professing it, and
demonstrating it publicly are two different things.
Conservative Christians have failed to do their homework. We have left the critical fields of philosophy,
history, anthropology, and the social sciences to
biblically uncommitted and even antichristian scholar-
ship. The results of this surrender are proving cata-
strophic. Nothing short of a Christian reformation can
alter the direction of the stream. But the change must
be brought about. But it will not be done without
sweat and tears. Proof texts and slogans will arouse
the saints but will not win the battle. If the Christian
gospel is to regain a position of authority in shaping
the form of our culture, a great deal of hard work is
ahead for us. To fight the good fight of faith requires
a good deal more intellectual sinews and muscles than
most Christians realize.

The apostle Paul explained his strategy for personal evangelism in the words "all things to all men"
(1 Co 9:22). He meant to imply nothing of the modern notion of relativism which today would be attached to such a slogan. His faith in the historical
truthfulness and doctrinal content of the gospel is well
known. His emphasis lay in another direction. Effective evangelism requires a personal accommodation
without compromise of truth to the total situation of
men. In his own life Paul showed tremendous ver-

satility getting alongside people from various backgrounds. He was able to communicate the data of the gospel with maximum effect because he showed himself willing to understand his audience. To the slave he became a slave, to the Jew a Jew, to the Roman a Roman. His strategy of personal empathy and understanding is relevant today. We need to make a conscious effort to comprehend the darkness outside of Christ. A complacent, bourgeois church cannot do this. The agony and tears of the secular prophets must be shared if we are to convince them of the pertinence of the gospel. Our age is vastly overrated. The common opinion that man has come of age is contrary to all empirical tests except the advance in technology which may yet destroy us all. Morally and spiritually man is still an infant. Historic Christianity can be effectively preached in the twentieth century. The new theologies will pass away because they seek to rescue the perishing by sinking the lifeboat. Yet the biblical faith will not gain a hearing in our culture until Christians shake off their cultural apathy and engage themselves in the debates of our time. Nor is it a matter only of accommodation to the intellectual and spiritual currents of our day. There needs to be a personal and corporate demonstration in the church of the existence of God and the truth of the gospel. The Christian life is posited upon the reality of biblical truth. The normal Christian life ought to contain powerful proofs for the gospel in the form of answered prayer and clear direction. Too much of orthodox Protestantism is spiritually dead. It trusts as much in carnal methods and procedures as men of the world do. Small wonder men have not found its message credible. Our evidence will not be accepted so long as our lives are not authentic. The greatest

hindrance to the spread of the gospel is the shallow-
ness of Christians. Men are deterred from considering
Christ because our lives are unreal and false. God's
men for this hour must be transparently genuine,
committed and convinced.

The task of Christian apologetics is a serious one.
Let no one take it on without realizing the issues.
For while it can be life unto life, it can also be death
unto death (2 Co 2:14). When the Pharisees were
confronted with unmistakable proofs of Jesus' divinity,
they hardened their hearts further, and blasphemed
against the Holy Spirit (Mt 12:22-32). Jesus Himself
warned that an awareness of His person and work
increases the responsibility of men regarding their
spiritual position (Jn 15:24). It is a sobering thought
to recognize the tragic results that can ensue from
effective apologetics. "If any man come to me, and
hate not . . . his own life also, he cannot be my
disciple" (Lk 14:26). The cost of discipleship to
Jesus Christ is dear in the field of apologetics. It will
be measured in hours of exhausting discussion, in
harsh words of studied contempt, in personal incon-
venience and discomfort. But He who said, "Ye shall
be witnesses unto me" (Ac 1:8), also said, "Lo, I
am with you alway, even unto the end of the world"
(Mt 28:18).

APPENDIX

ON METHOD IN CHRISTIAN
APOLOGETICS

SINCE IT APPEARED in 1967, *Set Forth Your Case* has received a wide and generous response. What is chiefly required of this edition is a further explication and exhibition of the theoretical structure underlying the argument. An iceberg is only partially visible; most of it lies beneath the surface. In this appendix we explore the intellectual basis which undergirds the book's thesis.

Set Forth Your Case has two major thrusts. First, it is alarmed at the disengagement from history which modern theology has for some time allowed and encouraged. The essence and beauty of the Christian message lie in its historical objectivity. Several details need to be added to fill out this conviction somewhat. Second, the book engages in what might be termed "cultural apologetics." The inexorable, logical and historical direction of secular humanism is toward inevitable and humanly insoluble dilemmas. The purpose of these lines is not so much to add to the avalanche of evidence that answers are not forthcoming from within the human situation of life's questions, as to analyze more carefully what we are doing when we relate the gospel to the contemporary intellectual climate. The Christian community desperately needs a new generation of committed scholars who are not intellectually intimidated and stubbornly refuse

to abandon the truth field to secularism. One purpose
of this book is to encourage the rise of the new breed
of dedicated apologists by indicating an exciting and
sound program to follow.

Revelation as History

A sad feature of Christianity today is the intellectual
intimidation of the faithful. Finding themselves in-
capable of defending belief against skeptical attack,
they retreat from the field of combat into the quaran-
tined security of pure subjectivity. The retreat to self-
authenticating, existential faith is not only cowardly
but also traitorous because Christianity is essentially
a religion of *factual belief*. The Christian message
does not call for blind credulity. Faith is a grounded
conviction, securely based upon objective revelation
data, which it is our solemn responsibility to present
and defend. We emphatically disassociate ourselves
from the Kantian revolution in the philosophy of
religion which would segregate religious language from
cognitive truth. The disastrous faith-versus-knowledge
epistemology of both liberal and neoorthodox theology
is to be discarded on both biblical and logical grounds.

The bane of modern theology has been the insistence that the acts of God are visible only to the
eyes of faith, and the Word of God is never to be
identified with any given text. No more consistent
advocate of faith as bare decision, entirely unrelated
to any factual state of affairs, exists than Rudolf Bultmann. While he freely admits that the New Testament
regards the resurrection of Christ to count for miraculous attestation of the divinity of Jesus, he regards
such an idea as fatal. He would contend that the saving Christ-event is not recognizable as such apart from
prior nonrational commitment to it. A less strident

form of this neognosticism is found in Karl Barth. For him Jesus comes *incognito*. He has no authenticating credentials. Faith is a closed circle without bridges to the public areas of human knowledge and truth. Although in theology Barth retains, as Bultmann does not, a profound loyalty to biblical content, he does not have more to offer us in the sphere of apologetics than Bultmann does. No doubt the dialectical theologians are moved by a certain fear that secular criticism may shake the citadel of faith. However, they fail to see that the alternative they present spells only mysticism and chaotic subjectivity. We will not save the Christian faith by denying the Christian facts. In their own ways, Cornelius Van Til and Gordon Clark further encourage the disengagement from history in their advocacy of presuppositional apologetics. Here too we are told that the facts of redemptive history are not accessible until after a commitment to the Christian position has been secured. This not only leaves us with no possible way to distinguish a true commitment from a false one, but is fundamentally incompatible with the apostolic appeal to what God *did.* as a basis for what men ought to *believe.*

The disengagement from history in modern theology has contributed to the rise of secularism. By agreeing that God is not truly revealed in ordinary secular history and thus not effectively challenging the naturalistic reading of history, the theologians have failed both to stem the secular conquest of the truth field and to make their case meaningful. If the acts of God are only faith events, then they are on any sensible assessment *pseudo-events*. Before Christians talk about revelation *in* history, they must decide whether they really mean that. If they do, as they ought, then they must face the fact that their assertions will have to be defended. When these theologians contend that the acts of God are nonobjective, they are talking non-sense. If all they mean by "acts of God" is a sub-jective event in personal experience, they end up in the same vicious, subjectivity circle that Schleiermacher operated in. But if they really mean more—that God did act redemptively in history, but in such a way that the fact can in no manner be verified in the public domain—then they are making no sense at all. This deep, internal inconsistency in neoorthodox thought is a major cause of its present decline and of the profound ferment in contemporary theology.

The importance of the historical evidence we have cited in this book lies in the clue it provides to the nature of ultimate reality. God has set up signposts on the landscape of created being which point beyond it to Him. The resurrection, for example, demonstrates what should, and ultimately will, concern man ulti-mately. It points to a divine solution to the human predicament which comes from beyond the flux, to an extraterrestial Archemedian point, which lends order and significance to everything else. If the Christian claim is not true, it is difficult to see how man can ever escape smothering relativity and arrive at life's meaning.

There is today, however, a widespread pessimism about man's ability to transcend his own finite situa-tion or presuppositions and arrive at objective find-ings. It is held by the existential historians that sub-ject and object are virtually indistinguishable and that the initial starting point, sovereignly chosen, is decisive. The unhappy consequence of this position is to make history pliable to whatever decision we happen to make, whether we be Marxist, Nazi, or Epicurean.

The result is chaotic solipsism and the end to progress in learning. Indeed, it enables the sinful subject to bend reality in his own direction and elude its force. Fortunately such pessimism is unwarranted. While it is true that a historical question has several possible answers, it does not have so many *probable* ones. It is possible that Jesus was a charlatan, as Schonfield says, but it is hardly probable. Any given opinion is subject to the constraint of the evidence. We must responsibly sift and weigh the data and come to a decision that seems most likely. Christians hold that Jesus Christ is the clue to universal history as well as individual lives. We confidently invite others to examine the evidence carefully because we are convinced that it points in the direction of faith in Jesus.

We do not claim for this evidence analytic or absolute certainty. The assurance is of a different kind. All legal and moral decisions are founded upon sound, empirical probabilities. The historical evidence is, in our opinion, sufficient to render men without excuse for not availing themselves of the free gift of God. There are powerful incentives to become Christians. It is the primary, positive task of Christian apologetics to set forth these grounds.

Cultural Apologetics

Cultural expressions in literature and the arts are a revelation of what lies in the heart of man. A novel may not have a thesis, but it will have a premise. It will indicate the author's vision of reality, the ultimate concern which he treasures. Cultural forms are a commentary upon the self-understanding of a generation. They are inescapably religious; that is, they already represent an essentially religious response to existence. Art depicts the spiritual situation of the artist. It poses from the human side the mystery of human life which only divine answers can resolve.

What precisely has taken place in our Western culture in these last decades? The humanistic hens have come home to roost! Secularity has set in with the result that what is "real" is the profane, a contingent world without purpose, and smothering relativity. Camus wrote,

> Up til now, man derived his coherence from his Creator. But from the moment that he consecrates his rupture with Him, he finds himself delivered over to the fleeting moment, to the passing days, and to wasted sensibility.[1]

The notion that human life and history have *a* purpose is a religious one. The logical conclusion from the secular premises is that life is set in an impersonal and purposeless matrix, and can offer only temporal purposes, games of distraction. It is curious why people on the whole are not ready to buy that idea. Surely, if they are indeed the products of chance evolution, they would have adapted themselves to the lack of transcendent purpose. Do fish complain that the sea is wet? The Bible explains that the reason people do not feel altogether at home in this world is that they were made for another.

In 1969 the Nobel prize for literature went to Samuel Beckett. Beckett's entire work has been termed a sermon on a remark about his ideology by James Joyce: "Here is life without God. Just look at it!" For Beckett, men wait in passive squalor for nothing. His plays articulate a theme running throughout modern literature. Writing today is largely based upon the absence of God. Beckett is what the twentieth century deserves. Such a premise could only bring about a radical transformation in sensibility and

values. This is the real revolution of our time. The
universe bereft of the Divine is reduced to a bare,
alien, desolate world of mechanical causation. Men
may be free to choose, but what significance has any
choice they might make in a world infected with absurdity? At first, freedom in a godless world seemed
exhilarating, but soon it was seen to be a frightening
and futile gesture. For what lasting purpose should he
use his freedom? For mankind? What was there to
bind him in sacral obligation to his kind? His godless
freedom has rewarded him with metaphysical nausea.
Two times anything equals zero, according to Beckett.

The Bible knows a book with this sort of message
—Ecclesiastes. That book contends that no matter
how wealthy or how wise a man may be, his life is
without ultimate significance or value in and of itself.
If man is all there is, and if nature is a closed system
of material cause and effect, then history is pointless
and life absurd. Only in relation to God can human
existence be beautiful. Sartre puts his finger on the
problem:

> All kinds of materialism lead one to treat every
> man including oneself as an object—that is, as a set
> of predetermined reactions, in no way different from
> the patterns of qualities and phenomena which con-
> stitute a table or a chair or a stone.[2]

Finitism is nihilism. Matter plus time chance equal
zero. The logic is as irrefutable as it is deadly.

Cultural apologetics intends to focus upon the
dilemmas of man as he himself expresses them. It
takes its point of departure in the cultural media and
seeks to pinpoint the fundamental difficulty. Even
Beckett is of the greatest value to the Christian witness. Just as white mice used to be taken down in
submarines because their noses became sensitive to

poison vapors before the crew's were, in an analogous
fashion Beckett has a good nose! He is adept at
sniffing out the deadly fumes of man-centered thought
before other men do. He is a kind of prophet, in the
sense that he speaks on behalf of his culture, and
that he is a premonition of things to come. Christians
have a responsibility to understand their culture. They
are sent by one who renounced the familiar divine
milieu and took up residence in the midst of sinful
people. Jesus Christ has demonstrated that it is possible to penetrate culture without being assimilated by
it. Scripture forbids us to love the world, but commands to understand it. Killinger is right:

> When the church fails to listen to contemporary
> art, it usually misses the temper and mood of hu-
> manity, and loses its opportunity to deal with the
> needs of man at the point where it might most
> readily have entered into them.[3]

And there are rich personal rewards as well. "By uni-
versalizing ourselves in the significant experience of
others, there is more of us that is Christian, that can
be Christian, than there was before."[4] Culturally barren Christians are no advertisement for the gospel. By
keeping aware of what is happening in the world
around, we ourselves become spiritually and mentally
bigger people. New horizons open, and there is more
of *us* to be Christian with!

The three distinguishing characteristics of our
secular mentality are relativism, positivism and secularism. *Relativism* holds that everything is in flux, all
knowledge is sociologically determined, all values are
shifting opinion. *Positivism* contends that material
reality is the only kind there is, that everything is
ruled by physical causation, and that religion and
ethics are non-sense. *Secularism* holds that the world

is intelligible on its own terms without reference to any reality beyond it. These three perspectives are on a rising curve. They are the logical result of humanistic premises, and therefore cannot be effectively challenged until those premises are overthrown. The central difficulty is the so-called "human predicament." Man lacks any absolute perspective from which to view the whole and find unity to his experience. The Christian faith is the ideal answer to his dilemma. It proclaims the grace of God coming to man from *outside* the human situation. Thus relativism can be transcended because we hear a word from beyond the flux; positivism can be refuted because the divine one has shown Himself in the empirical realm; and secularism can be avoided. After all, the best way to understand this world is to learn of another. "Aim at heaven and you get the world thrown in; aim at earth and you'll get neither," says C. S. Lewis. If the gospel is true, then the solution is at hand. Every act in the human drama is meaningful because it occupies a unique place in God's plan. The sinfulness of man finds an answer in the atoning work of Jesus on the cross. All history is seen moving toward judgment. It is difficult to envisage a more beautiful and satisfying solution. And yet it is grounded, not in an idealistic imagination, but in historical reality.

Postscript

Jesus told His disciples that they were to be leaven and salt in the world. The Christian message is one which can save the world both historically and eschatologically. But enthusiasm is not enough. What is needed now is the emergence of a new generation of tough-minded Christian intellectuals. God is still asking, "Whom shall I send, and who will go for us?" (Is 6:8).

NOTES

Introduction

[1] Daniel Wilson, *The Evidences of Christianity* (Boston: Crocker & Brewster, 1829), p. 25.

Chapter 1

[1] B. B. Warfield in F. R. Beattie, *Apologetics* (Richmond, Va.: Presb. Com. of Publn., 1903), p. 25.

Chapter 3

[1] Bertrand Russell, *A Free Man's Worship* (Portland, Maine: Thomas Mosher, 1927), pp. 6-7.

[2] Richard Coe, *Samuel Beckett* (New York: Grove, 1964), p. 18.

Chapter 4

[1] Carl F. H. Henry, *The Drift of Western Thought* (Grand Rapids: Eerdmans, 1951), p. 12.

Chapter 5

[1] R. J. Rushdoony, *Intellectual Schizophrenia* (Nutley, N.J.: Presbyterian & Reformed, 1961), pp. 25 f.

Chapter 6

[1] Edward Gibbon, *Decline and Fall of the Roman Empire*, as cited by Peter L. Berger, *The Noise of Solemn Assemblies* (Garden City, N.J.: Doubleday, 1961), p. 68.

Chapter 7

[1] John W. Montgomery, *The Altizer-Montgomery Dialogue* (Chicago: Inter-Varsity, 1967), pp. 67 f.

Chapter 10

[1] C. S. Lewis, *Mere Christianity* (London: Fontana, 1952), pp. 52-53.

Chapter 15

[1] R. J. Rushdoony, *By What Standard* (Philadelphia: Presbyterian and Reformed, 1959), pp. 19 f.

[2] John W. Montgomery, *The Altizer-Montgomery Dialogue* (Chicago: Inter-Varsity, 1967), pp. 21 f.

[3] Ibid.

Appendix

[1] Albert Camus, *The Rebel* (New York: Knopf, 1954), p. 47.

[2] Jean-Paul Sartre, *Communists and Peace,* ed. Philip R. Berk (New York: Braziller, 1968).

[3] John Killinger, *Failure of Theology in Modern Literature* (New York: Abingdon, 1963), p. 15.

[4] Henry Zylstra, *Testament of Vision* (Grand Rapids: Eerdmans, 1958), p. 57.

A SELECTIVE BIBLIOGRAPHY FOR CHRISTIAN APOLOGETICS

Armerding, Hudson T. *Christianity and the World of Thought*. Chicago: Moody, 1968.

Babbage, Stuart B. *The Mark of Cain*. Grand Rapids: Eerdmans, 1966.

Berger, Peter L. *A Rumour of Angels: Modern Society and the Rediscovery of the Supernatural*. Garden City, N.Y.: Doubleday, 1969.

Bruce, Frederick F. *New Testament Documents: Are They Reliable?* Chicago: Inter-Varsity, 1943.

Carnell, Edward J. *An Introduction to Christian Apologetics*. Grand Rapids: Eerdmans, 1955.

Fuller, Daniel P. *Easter Faith and History*. Grand Rapids: Eerdmans, 1965.

Gerstner, John H. *Reasons for Faith*. Grand Rapids: Baker, 1960.

Gilkey, Langdon. *Naming the Whirlwind: The Renewal of God-Language*. Indianapolis: Bobbs-Merrill, 1969.

Hamilton, Kenneth. *Revolt Against Heaven*. Grand Rapids: Eerdmans, 1965.

Hanson, Anthony, ed. *Vindications: Essays on the Historical Basis of Christianity*. New York: Morehouse-Barlow, 1966.

Harrison, Roland K. *Introduction to the Old Testament*. Grand Rapids: Eerdmans, 1969.

Henry, C. F. H. *Giving a Reason for Our Hope*. Natick, Mass.: Wilde, 1949.

———. *Remaking the Modern Mind*. Grand Rapids: Eerdmans, 1948.

Kitchen, Kenneth A. *Ancient Orient and Old Testament.*
Chicago: Inter-Varsity, 1966.
Klotz, John W. *Genes, Genesis, and Evolution.* St. Louis:
Concordia, 1955.
Lewis, C. S. *Mere Christianity.* London: Fontana, 1952.
————. *Miracles.* New York: Collins, 1947.
Lightner, Robert. *The Saviour and the Scriptures.* Nutley,
N.J.: Presbyterian & Reformed, 1965.
Little, Paul E. *How to Give Away Your Faith.* Chicago:
Inter-Varsity, 1966.
Mollenkott, Virginia R. *Adamant and Stone-Chips.* Waco,
Tex.: Word, 1967.
Monsma, John C. *Evidence of God.* New York: Putnam,
1958.
Montgomery, John W. *The 'Is God Dead?' Controversy.*
Grand Rapids: Zondervan, 1966.
————. *The Shape of the Past.* Ann Arbor: Edwards,
1962.
————. *Where Is History Going?* Grand Rapids: Zonder-
van, 1969.
Morrison, F. *Who Moved the Stone?* London: Faber &
Faber, 1958.
Nash, Ronald. *The Philosophy of Gordon H. Clark.*
Nutley, N.J.: Presbyterian & Reformed, 1968.
Orr, J. Edwin. *The Christian View of God and the World.*
New York: Scribner, 1897.
Phillips, J. B. *The Ring of Truth.* New York: Mac-
millan, 1967.
Pinnock, Clark H. *A Defense of Biblical Infallibility.*
Nutley, N.J.: Presbyterian & Reformed, 1967.
Plantinga, Alvin. *God and Other Minds.* Ithaca, N.Y.:
Cornell U., 1967.
Ramm, Bernard. *Protestant Christian Evidences.* Chicago:
Moody, 1953.
————. *Varieties of Christian Apologetics.* Grand Rapids:
Baker, 1961.
Sherwin-White, A. N. *Roman Society and Roman Law
in the New Testament.* Oxford: U. Press, 1963.

Smith, Wilbur M. *Therefore Stand*. Grand Rapids: Baker, 1969.

Stott, John R. *Basic Christianity*. Grand Rapids: Eerdmans, 1957.

Trueblood, Elton. *A Place to Stand*. New York: Harper & Row, 1969.

Wilder-Smith, A. E. *Man's Origin, Man's Destiny*. Wheaton, Ill.: Shaw, 1968.

Zylstra, Henry. *Testament of Vision*. Grand Rapids: Eerdmans, 1958.